GRANITE

FIZZ

GRANITE FIZZ

*The Untold Story of Spring Water and
Flavored Tonic in New Hampshire*

Dennis Sasseville

ISBN 979-8-9876986-0-0
Library of Congress Control Number: 2023910673

Published by Wellfleet Associates
Bedford, New Hampshire; Third Printing

All photographs credited to Dennis Sasseville unless otherwise noted.

Visit: www.granitefizz.com

Printed in the United States of America.

Dedicated to six marvelous grandchildren who share my love for both New England tonics and great-tasting spring water: Caleb, Andrew, Natalie, Hannah, Anna, and Michelle.

TABLE OF CONTENTS

INTRODUCTION

And, occasionally, on red-letter days, as Cousin Alfred and I
took our leave, Mr. Wiley would call after us. "Hot, ain't it?
Why don't you boys have a bottle of cold tonic 'fore you go?"
And he would let us select from among the bottles of birch
beer, root beer, sarsaparilla, ginger ale, Moxie, lemon, lime,
orange, raspberry and vanilla soda packed in ice in a big
wooden tub.[1]

Yes, the author quoted above is writing about a remembrance from the Bay
State, but the scene could just as easily have been any small New Hampshire
town in the post-World War II years. Call it soda, pop, or tonic. Just
consuming one today can evoke fond memories of a summer's ice-cold
refreshment enjoyed at a sandy ocean beach, a picnic on a grassy hill, laying
on your back on a freshy mowed backyard lawn, or just standing on the street
corner outside of the neighborhood corner store with a school friend. In
those instances, the beverage in your hand seems much more substantial
than just colored, flavored, sugary, fizzy water. And that *substantial nostalgia*
helps maintain our fondness for the simple pleasure of a favorite flavored

carbonated soft drink. We don't typically attach such personal feelings to a bottle of spring water, however pure and refreshing or nutritionally superior it might be.

In the United States alone, since 1825, more than 30,000 soft drink bottlers have created and sold "fizzy" soft drinks to everyday consumers. Amazingly, those companies produced in excess of 16,000 different brands and drink names–most of which survive only as part of our collective memories or known only to the most ardent memorabilia collectors. It was the golden age of remedies, elixirs, and tonics in the latter half of the 19th century that helped to pioneer American's thirst for non-alcoholic (or soft) beverages and led to their consumer-fueled explosion after 1900.

> When traveling the main highways of this country, when attending a game in a ball park, or while watching TV, America's thirst is quenched by the one and only soda pop industry. Have you ever gone more than 50 miles without the children begging for a soft drink?
> Source: Ferraro and Ferraro, 1964.

Soft drinks, carbonated or not, start with something absolutely basic to our blue planet – water. Water is of course integral to the making of all types of beverages. But it also is a commodity unto itself. The first commercial bottled water in this country reportedly took place in 1767 in Boston. In the 19th century Saratoga Springs, New York, as well as Poland Spring, Maine, successfully created destination resorts and water empires. From that modest start in 18th century Boston, Americans would regularly consume more bottled water than any other packaged beverage by 2017. Sales of bottled waters in the United States exceeded forty-six gallons per person in 2021 and are still rising.

The Northeast section of the United States played a large role in the development and promotion of both spring waters and carbonated flavored beverages. New Hampshire's role in what became an expansive American industry has perhaps been proportionately smaller but by no means inconsequential. New Hampshire has hosted at least 205 carbonated soda and spring water bottlers, representing locations in some sixty cities and towns, from the mid-1800s up through today. This number is quite likely an undercount, as a review of historic city directories and various health department inspection reports reflects many more small, often short-term enterprises for which embossed glass bottles and product delivery records no longer exist.

The following chapters will explore the roots of the soft drink and water bottling industries and the Granite State's historic and current role in these mega commercial beverage sectors that seem to touch all of our lives in one fashion or another. From Nutfield's Blood Orange soda (Derry) to Lucky Strike's Ginger Ale (Nashua) to today's Coca-Cola Zero Sugar (Londonderry) and Squamscot's Maple Cream (Newfields), New Hampshire reflects a rich and diverse offering of flavored tonics.

First, perhaps a word on some operating definitions to set the stage for the chapters to follow.

SOFT DRINKS OR SOFT BEVERAGES

These can be any type of non-alcoholic liquid beverage. A side note: any type of fermented beverage, or concentrate used in the making of a beverage, will undoubtedly contain some alcohol, even in trace amounts. The fermentation process consumes sugars and produces CO_2 and some alcohol. This is how beers get their fizz and their alcohol content. So yes, a fermented root beer soda likely contains a smidgeon of alcohol.

SODA, POP, COKE, TONIC, SOFT DRINK

These are all common terms for flavored carbonated non-alcoholic beverages, but whose specific term depends largely on your cultural traditions and region of the country. Most of us on the East and West coasts use the term *soda*, but Mid-westerners tend to call it *pop* and many Southerners will ask for either a *coke, cocola*, or a *soft drink. Tonic* is generally restricted to eastern Massachusetts, especially the Boston area, but New Hampshirites and Mainers have been known to adopt this handle as well. It is an old-school term, as greater than 30 percent of Massachusetts residents born in the 1940s say *tonic* but almost none of the younger generation does.

WATER

You might think that water would be a simple medium to classify–it's not. Spring water, Sparkling water, Mineral water, Live water? This is especially true when we consider the modern market for bottled water products and how they are regulated in commerce. And of course, water is a primary component of soft drinks as well.

In modern times the U.S. Food and Drug Administration (FDA) regulates commercially bottled water products for the safety and health of the American public. Logically, the FDA classifies water by its origin or source:

> **Artesian well water**—This water is collected from a well that taps an aquifer—layers of porous rock, sand, and earth that contain water—which is under pressure from surrounding upper layers of rock or clay. When tapped, the pressure in the aquifer, commonly called artesian pressure, pushes the water to the surface.

> **Mineral water**—This water comes from an underground source and contains at least 250 parts per million total

dissolved solids (TDS) in a fairly constant concentration and proportion. Minerals and trace elements must come from the geologic source of the underground water - they cannot be added during processing.

Spring water—Derived from an underground formation from which water flows naturally to the surface, this water must be collected only at the spring or through a well that taps the underground formation feeding the spring. If extracting the water through a well, the water must have the same composition and quality as the water that flowed naturally to the land surface.

Well water—This is water from a hole bored or drilled well into the ground, which taps into a bedrock or surficial aquifer that can be extracted (pumped). Common to New England terminology, bedrock-drilled wells are referred to as *artesian wells*, even when not truly artesian in nature.

Municipal water—In common terms, we're talking tap water here. The water's origin may be from a surface reservoir or groundwater extraction wells, or a blend. As delivered, it is typically pre-treated to remove sediment, color, or other unwanted materials. It is most often chlorinated, and possibly fluoridated, before delivered to the point of use for consumption.

Water from any of the above sources may be commercially bottled for public consumption. The FDA regulations have additional stipulations concerning the required production conditions during the handling, storage and bottling processes, and ultimately the standard of quality (chemical, physical and microbiological) for the finished water offered to the public.

These federal requirements are reinforced, and often surpassed, by individual state and local governmental requirements.

But we're not quite done with terms and definitions for this humble substance – water. Bottled consumer beverages that are labeled as *sparking water, seltzer water, soda water, club soda* or *tonic water* are NOT considered waters by the FDA, but rather are formally classified as soft drinks.

> **Sparkling water**—often a general term for any type of water that is carbonated.
>
> **Seltzer**—any carbonated water without anything further additives.
>
> **Soda water or club soda**—carbonated water with minerals added (commonly sodium).
>
> **Tonic water**—carbonated water with quinine added for flavor.
>
> **Still water**—uncarbonated water (not typically bottled but served directly in eating establishments, on airlines, etc.). In most cases the origin is local tap water.

Further distinctions among these familiar beverage categories as well as their origins and paths of evolution are explored as we procedure through the next six chapters of this book.

1 THE EARLY CONSUMPTION AND MARKETING OF NATURAL WATERS

In the 17th and 18th century Europe, natural spring waters were very much in vogue–both for bathing and drinking. The natural bubbling spring water discovered in the Belgian town of Spa was believed to have healing powers, thus resorts and healing centers built around such springs were commonly called *spas*. The term, as used today, still harkens back to these healing roots, but it is employed with broader applications to wellness and a host of personal body-care activities.

Monks from the Great Malvern Priory in the United Kingdom began bottling and locally distributing drinkable healing waters from their famed Holy Well in 1622. Water magnate-to-be Jacob Schweppe, who had patented a process for artificially creating mineral waters in 1783, began commercializing the Malvern Waters in 1843 (1850 by some accounts). He introduced the water as Malvern Soda, renaming it Malvern Seltzer Water in 1856. His bottled unflavored natural product was distributed throughout

England with great success, launching a family bottling enterprise that continues to the present.

Spring water was also the subject of great interest in the 18th century American colonies from progressive physicians interested in the health aspect. Two prominent physician-researchers in the colonies were Dr. Benjamin Rush of Philadelphia and Dr. Benjamin Waterhouse of the Harvard Medical School. Spring water also captured the interests of many of our budding country's statemen-scientists, including James Madison, Thomas Jefferson and John Adams. For instance, Jefferson commented extensively in his 1781 writings on the medicinal potential of Virginia's natural springs.

> Between 1773 and 1785 there were a number of prominent American scientists and statesmen investigating naturally- effervescent (carbonated) mineral waters. This group included two future U.S. Presidents: Thomas Jefferson and James Madison.
> Source: Riley, 1972.

Closer to New England, Sir William Johnson, Major-General of the British Army was reported as the first European to visit the mineral-rich Saratoga Springs[2] in New York in 1755, having been directed there by Native Americans. Mohawk and Iroquois tribes would reportedly partake of the many springs there for both drinking and bathing. Johnson recognized the health benefits of the naturally carbonated springs and later wrote on the subject to his friend, General Philip Schuyler, a Patriot officer and Albany native. In 1783, Schuyler directed George Washington to visit Saratoga Springs while in the area so he could observe the special waters first-hand. The following year, a friend of Washington's also investigated the springs and wrote back to him:

…But what distinguishes these waters in a very conspicuous degree from all others, is the great quantity of fixed air (carbon dioxide) which they contain. They are exceedingly pungent to the taste, and after being drunk a short time will often affect the nose like brisk bottled ale. …Several persons told us that they had corked it (the waters) tight in bottles, and that the bottles broke.

Subsequent investigations by other scientists and physicians furthered the knowledge of naturally-carbonated waters, which originate in subsurface layers of shale rock along a north-south geologic fault zone in the Sarasota area. By 1823 entrepreneurs were bottling the Mohawk's "Medicine Waters of the Great Spirit" under several different brand names. That year English emigrant "Doctor" John Clarke (an honorary title) and a partner established a bottling plant, and by 1826 they were bottling 1200 bottles a day from the springs. From that point on into the 20th century, Saratoga Springs continued to evolve into a prime American destination spa in the mold of the famous European establishments. Saratoga Springs bottled water can still be purchased far and wide today.

> In old New England an "Adam's ale" was a term used for good spring water that flowed year around – a reference to a perfectly innocent drink from the Garden of Eden.
> Source: Farrow, 1985.

* * *

THE NEW ENGLAND EXPERIENCE

New England's first reported commercial offering of bottled water was at Jackson's Spa in Boston in 1767—nearly ten years before the country started on the road to becoming the independent United States. The exact location and duration of the Jackson Spa is unclear, but may have been just south of Boston, in the Jamacia Plain area[3]. Settlers in New England typically chose locations that were suited to water transportation and commerce; they also were mindful to ensure access to clean and abundant drinking water. Thus, it was common to select a settlement location based on the availability of a dependable spring or stream. Almost universally, the first New England colonists described the region's water as being soft and "sweet" (i.e., low in dissolved mineral matter). Soils and surficial deposits in New England are primarily derived from glaciation over terrain, exposing hard granitic and metamorphic rock, with very little limestone or marble to impart a hardness to the natural waters.

> Isn't all water "Mineral Water?" Technically, yes, all water, even rain water will contain some dissolved minerals unless it's been highly distilled. But for consumer purposes the U.S. FDA defines Minerals Waters as having come from an underground source that naturally contains at least 250 parts per million of total dissolved solids (i.e., minerals).
> Source: USGS.

As the country matured, the American public's interest in bottled water from springs or spas[4] continued to grow. This was partly due to the perceived direct health benefits achieved by the consumption of such waters, and also as a preferred alternative to the often-suspect quality and reliability of municipally-supplied drinking waters. The launching of the New England bottled water industry can be traced to a religious sect, the Shakers, located in a lightly-settled area of the interior of southern Maine.

The Shakers, more formally known as the United Society of Believers in Christ's Second Appearing, established more than twenty communities of believers in the eastern United States, starting in the late 18th century. At least four organized communities were started in southern Maine in the 1780s and 1790s: Alfred, Gorham, Poland, and New Gloucester. Only the Alfred (Shaker Hill) and New Gloucester (Sabbathday Lake) communities were to experience any longevity[5].

As with the other communities, Sabbathday Lake strove to be as self-sufficient as possible while still interacting with their surrounding communities and the world at large. They sold produce from their farms and commercial goods from their mills. Like many of their sister communities, Sabbathday Lake also sold garden seeds in packets as well as bottled medicinal products (more on the subject of Shaker medicinals in Chapter 2).

While the celibate Shakers took in orphaned children and grew their ranks in that manner, it was quite common for adults to willingly join these communities, often including their entire families. In doing so they brought with them all their worldly goods to be contributed to the communal Shaker way of life.

When the Shakers came to Poland, Maine in 1783, local farmer Eliphaz Ring converted to Shakerism along with his wife and children[6]. As was customary, Ring then turned the ownership of his 300-acre property over to his new community of fellow believers. Fifty miles or so south of Poland the elders of the Alfred Shaker community wanted a saw and grist mill site owned by a local, Jabez Ricker. Ricker had little interest in joining the religious sect, so the Elders offered him the larger Ring property in Poland in exchange for his, along with 450 British pounds "lawful money." That sealed the deal, and the Ricker family packed up their possessions and moved to their new farm in Poland in 1794, renaming Ring Hill to Ricker Hill.

One major benefit to the newly-acquired Ricker property was a clear free-flowing spring that graced the hillside. The natural spring had long been known to the area's Native Americans but son Wentworth Ricker enhanced the source by creating a channel and trough so his cattle could drink freely of the pure water. Over the decades both family members and neighbors claimed relief from kidney troubles or dyspepsia through drinking the farm's pure spring water. Jabez Ricker's grandson, Hiram, thought to capitalize on his family's healing waters, and through a neighbor he learned of a certain Portland physician. Hiram visited the physician and convinced him to use the Rickers' spring water to treat one of his patients who was suffering from "kidney hemorrhages." The patient improved, and so impressed was the good doctor that he placed a standing order with Hiram for a 5-gallon spring water delivery twice a week so he could dispense portions to his patients.

That initial patient was so pleased with his resulting health benefit that he entered into a partnership with Hiram to develop the spring commercially. The Ricker farm's scenic country location along with the growing reputation of the natural spring brought the traveling public to Ricker Hill. In 1860 the Poland Spring resort destination and the water sales business were off and running and would soon take the country by storm. New England would now have a spa resort and spring water distribution system to rival both Saratoga Springs and the European experiences.

The Shakers still owned some property in Poland, including some lands adjacent to the Ricker Farm. The growing notoriety of the Ricker's business venture led the Shaker community to market their version of Poland Mineral

Springs Medicinal Water starting around 1860. Perhaps the Shaker community's advertising approach was just not robust enough, but their efforts were apparently unsuccessful. In contrast, the Maine Shaker's sister community in Harvard, Massachusetts sold bottled water from their on-site spring under the clever tagline of "Moses smote the Rock. This Water smites Disease and Death." The fact that most members of the Harvard Shaker community lived well into their 90s was a seemingly-strong substantiation of the product's beneficial health claims. No doubt many of the locals took note and eagerly purchased the Shaker's spring water to secure their own good health and longevity.

* * *

THE GRANITE STATE

New Hampshire certainly had a wealth of natural springs and some notable sales of spring water products, but nothing on the scale and success of either Poland Spring or Saratoga Springs. Early New Hampshire springs were discovered and exploited in the 19th century to various degrees in Amherst, Bradford, Charlestown, Concord, Conway, Goffstown, Jaffrey, Littleton, Moultonborough, Pittsfield, Plaistow, Unity, Walpole and many other locales. Many of the identified springs were never fully commercialized but often supplied water to their communities through local distribution channels. Individuals were permitted to visit the spring location and fill their own containers for personal consumption back at their homes and farms. Naturally, some spring owners did attempt to serve a more expansive market, especially if the waters were thought to have medicinal or healing properties.

The United States Geological Survey (USGS) reported in 1899 that six New Hampshire springs were registering commercial sales of their products, a doubling from the previous water survey. A 1909 the Bureau of Mines report[7] on the mineral resources of the United States indicated that mineral waters sold in New Hampshire amounted to 934,072 gallons, an increase of greater than 11 percent over the previous year. The report listed ten commercial springs operating in the State, with water said to be "...principally for medicinal purposes. One of the springs is a resort, but at none is the water used for bathing. A considerable quantity of water was used in the manufacture of soft drinks." The reporting operations were:

> Cohas Spring, North Londonderry
> Granite State Spring, Plaistow
> Lafayette Mineral Spring, Derry
> Londonderry Lithia Well, Londonderry
> Mount Gunstock, Lake Shore Park (Belknap County)
> Mount Madison Spring, Gorham
> Pack Monadnock Lithia Spring, Temple
> White Mountain Mineral Spring, Conway
> Willow Spring, South Nashua
> Wilton Mineral Spring, Wilton

Other government reports of 1909 also list Hale Spring in Plaistow and Toof's Artesian Well in Concord. Clearly, the reporting on these types of state resources and commercial ventures often reflected data gaps and partial information.

Geologically, New Hampshire can draw upon two principal sources for obtaining large quantities of drinking water from its subsurface. The first source consists of sorted and layered outwash deposits left by the last glaciation, referred to as "stratified drift" by glacial geologists. The second water source is the underlying crystalline bedrock, especially where extensive fracturing or faults allow groundwaters to accumulate and flow.

What geologists call bedrock, old-time Yankees often called "ledge," a term still heard today in parts of the Granite State.

The glacial outwash deposits occur as fill in river valleys or lie like a blanket on the landscape where former glacial meltwaters and lakes stood during the waning of the last great ice age (approximately 12,000 years before present). Their sands, gravels and silty-clay layers are typically less than 100 feet thick but serve as excellent "sponges" for rainwater and localized runoff. These relict deposits provide dependable aquifers that can filter out most organic matter and surface contamination, yielding high-quality drinking waters.

Quality-wise, New Hampshire' glacial aquifers tend to produce "soft" water, that is slightly acidic and contains relatively low Total Dissolved Solids (TDS) (total dissolved mineral matter essentially). According two USGS studies of New Hampshire groundwaters, outwash deposits possess average (median) hardness or TSD levels between 22 and 37 parts per million (ppm). Any hardness value less than 60 ppm is considered soft water and the low amount of dissolved mineral matter results in a taste often referred to as "sweet" or "clean," especially when comparted to highly mineralized water.

Bedrock in the Granite State is predominately....well, granite. The State's foundation is dominated by hard igneous rock from the granite family and from associated formations that were baked by heat and pressure to crimp, squeeze, fold and mold them into durable underpinnings. This bedrock is composed primarily of "light" granites, those rich in silicate mineral like feldspar and quartz, and relatively low in "heavy" iron, manganese and magnesium minerals. Unlike our sister state of Vermont, New Hampshire is also fairly devoid of soluble calcareous deposits, like limestones or marbles. Those bedrock types are typically associated with hard water due to the abundance of dissolved calcium and magnesium. The USGS reports that New

Hampshire's mix of bedrock types yields groundwaters with a median hardness of about 65 ppm—considered moderately hard by water quality scientists.[8]

Of the numerous Granite State historical spring or mineral water operations, at least three locales warrant a closer look: the Milford Mineral Springs in Milford, the Cohas Spring in North Londonderry, and Lithia Springs in Londonderry. A fourth notable spring, Derry's Lafayette Mineral Spring, primarily supplied a soft-drink bottling operation and will be discussed in Chapters 4 and 5.

* * *

MILFORD MINERAL SPRINGS (PONEMAH SPRINGS)

The Milford Springs is tucked in the southeast corner of Milford on the slopes of Federal Hill and presumably the low alkaline springs emanate from the hard granite-gneiss bedrock in that area. The area borders the Ponemah[9] section of Amherst, and a series of destination hotels built on the site were universally called the Ponemah Hotel and advertised as such. Travelers coming from Boston and points south would depart their train at the Amherst station and take a short two-mile carriage ride to the hotel and spring complex. A hotel promotional brochure beckoned to the would-be traveler, "When the trees in September shall wear their varied tinted foliage a new charm will be added, and no more delightful place can be found to pass the coming month."

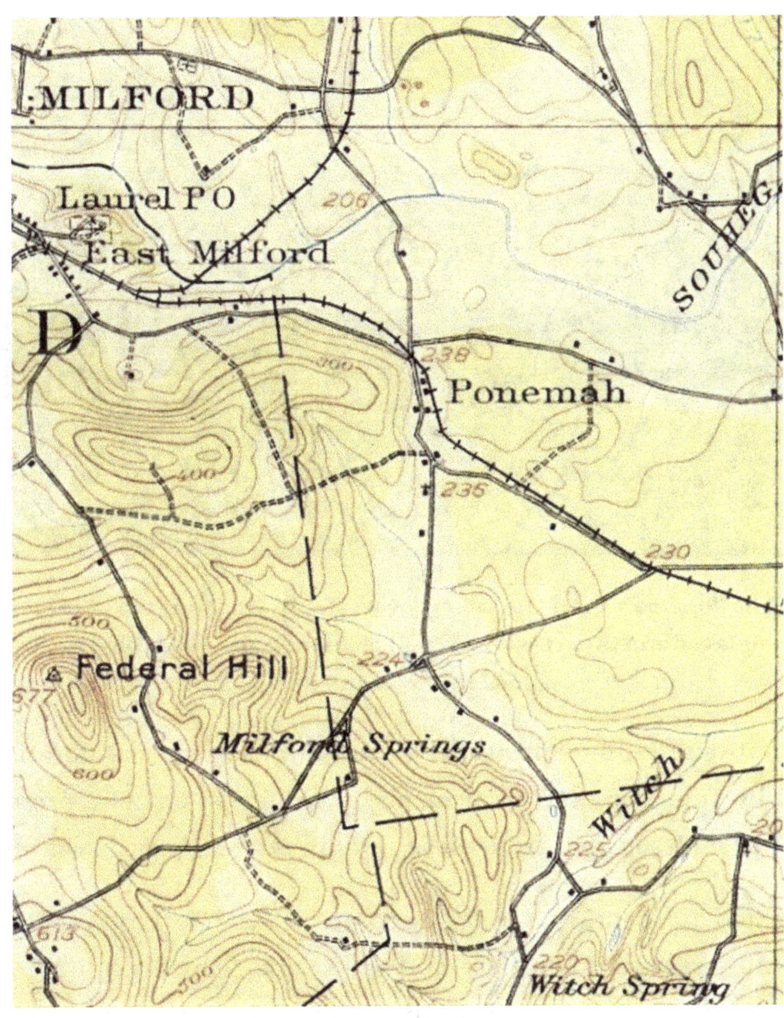

Illustration 1 On this 1906 USGS topographic map the Milford/Ponemah Springs are identified on Federal Hill (lower center). Visitors to the springs and hotel would often arrive at Amherst's Ponemah railroad station (center) and complete their journey via horse-drawn carriage.

Figure 1 The Ponemah Hotel from a 1915 post card. By this time the mineral springs were downplayed and the areas' vistas and pleasant countryside emphasized. A fire in 1921 consumed the hotel and it was not rebuilt.

In addition to printed postcards of the various hotel configurations that are held by collectors and local historical societies, an 1884 promotional brochure provides insights into these springs as a commercial venture.

In the late 19th century, the spring complex was referred to as "Ponemah and the Milford Mineral Springs" and was managed by the Milford Mineral Springs Co. from 161 Tremont St. in Boston. The company's promotional brochure cited a local knowledge of the Milford mineral springs and its curative benefits dating back to 1818. The brochure's proclamations include[10]:

...WE DO CLAIM that in the cure of all diseases caused by affected kidneys or disordered stomach, it is an invaluable aid and an indispensable adjunct to medical treatment, and as such is highly recommended by eminent physicians. ALSO,

That the PONEMAH is a natural spring.

That there is no purer water in the world.

That it is sparkling, very pleasant to the taste, and naturally charged with carbonic-acid gas.

That being entirely pure, and without a trace of vegetable contamination, it will keep unchanged for years.

That consequently, it is *unequaled* for the table by any water, whether from a natural spring or manufactured.

Not surprisingly, in promoting their pure product, the site owners refer to the often-disagreeable taste and odors of municipal-supplied waters and that that those waters were most suited "...for cleansing, and the many manufacturing processes..." But for heaven's sake, not for human consumption!

The 19th century-produced brochure contained the chemical analyses of the spring waters, and in a similar fashion to patent medicines of the day, offered an abundance of first-hand testimonies to both the pleasant taste of the effervescent waters, as well as their health benefits. One Dr. G.L. Austin provides the testimony:

There is no doubt that much of the mortality in the larger
cities is occasioned by the habitual use of pond or river water
… and people are becoming sensible, and are awakening to
the belief that in impurity lurks *disease* and *death.*

Four distinct springs were operating on the Ponemah site at this time:
Iron Spring, Magnesia Spring, Soda Spring, and the Milford Medical Spring.
Each contained a different mix of natural minerals and therefore were touted
as having different, but complementary, benefits. The on-site water bottling
operations may have drawn their water directly from any of these identified
sources, or perhaps they utilized a separate spring source site altogether.

The Ponemah spring water was referred to as the Acme of Table Waters
by the owners and was available bottled for $7 for a case of 50 quarts or $10
for a case of 100 pint. The company would also deliver a 40-gallon barrel of
spring water to any part of Boston for a mere $4 fee. Advertising of the day
touted wholesale agents in New York City and Cincinnati, Ohio who could
distribute the sparking Ponemah product, but it was also available from
leading grocers and druggists throughout the United States and Canada.
Sales numbers for this period are not known, nor is it certain when the
commercial sales of bottled waters from this Ponemah spring ceased.

As a hospitality venture, the Ponemah Hotel continued to operate under
various ownerships into the early 20th century. Travel literature of the time
drew attention to the view from the hotel grounds of the three celebrated
Ponemah and Milford Medicinal Mineral Springs, but only included a
passing reference to the water's health benefits. The new owners placed
decidedly more emphasis on the mountainside inn's spectacular vistas than
on the attributes of the site's spring waters.

Marketing brochures and even published gazettes of the period should not be counted on for accuracy (or perhaps even honesty). An 1839 New England Gazetteer lists the location of the Ponemah mineral springs at an 800 ft elevation. This would be quite the feat since the top of Milford's Federal Hill itself is 23 feet short of 700, and the hotel and springs are actually located farther down the hilly slopes at about 500 feet. The last of the grand hotels on this site burned in June 1921[11] and the springs are long-forgotten as a tourist destination or source of curative mineral waters. Located on heavily-wooded private land, at least one of the formerly-famous springs reportedly now serves as a welcomed respite for the owner's thirsty horses.

* * *

COHAS SPRINGS

In contrast to the bedrock-derived springs of the Milford Mineral Springs, the source of the Cohas Springs in North Londonderry were the extensive glacial outwash deposits that line a good portion of the Merrimack River Valley. These deposits originated during the waning of the last great glaciation in New England when ice dams in the Merrimack Valley formed huge but short-lived lakes where glacial sands and gravels could accumulate to sizable depths.

Glacial Lake Hooksett, north of Manchester, and glacial Lake Merrimack, extending from the Massachusetts border up to Manchester, were two of the larger features that date from approximately 6,000 years before present. Once the glacial meltwaters ceased and the ice dams broke, the Merrimack valley was left with thick, well-drained deposits, many now serving as source materials for sand and gravel mining operations used in highway and other construction activities. Such deposits are typically quite permeable to water flow and therefore serve as major drinking water aquifers (subsurface reservoirs) for many New Hampshire communities, as well as for various agricultural, industrial and, commercial uses.

These thick sand and gravel deposits can yield free-flowing springs of quite high quality and quantities, usually appearing in gullies or at the base of slopes. This was the case for the Cohas Springs, situated along Little Cohas Brook just due south of what is now the Manchester-Boston Regional Airport. Cohas Brook was first called Massabesic when surveyed in 1724 and then changed to Cohasset, or Cohassack, following the Native American term for "a place of pines" or "pine water." The location of the Manchester-Londonderry airport itself is no accident, but owes its 1927 founding to the relative flat-lying, well-drained, and easily worked glacial sand of the former Lake Merrimack.

The Cohas Springs[12] were apparently relatively short-lived as a viable, commercial water venture. Londonderry Town documents refer to a spring water complex founded by local businessman Roswell William Annis on September 16, 1907, as the Cohasaukee Corporation. The springs were reportedly capable of producing some 15,000 gallons a day of clear refreshment at a cool 41 degrees water temperature.

Illustration 2 In the early 1900s the Cohausaukee Corporation's packing room for its Cohas spring waters was a model for efficient bottling and distribution in its day. Credit: ImageAbility.

A 1908 company brochure[13] reflects a fully-functioning spring and gravity-fed bottling complex with carbonation equipment (indicating that these spring waters were not naturally carbonated) under the Cohasaukee Corporation. Founder Annis had grandiose plans for his piney Thousand Acre spread, including an amusement park to rival the nearby Pine Island Park and an extensive housing development. However, upon Annis' death in 1912, the Cohas Springs Bottling Plant was auctioned off in January 1913 with the expansive property divided into half a dozen separate parcels. The spring, along with the visitor's center, production and storage buildings and all machinery, were sold as one unit.

The Cohasaqua Corporation was subsequently formed in Manchester with new controlling ownership of the North Londonderry's spring and property. The company's 1913 legal filing listed $50,000 in capital stock to cover a host of business activities including, "…dealing in minerals and other waters and tonics, and bottling the same; developing the Cohas Spring water, and carrying on a general commercial business." The new corporation expanded operations and exported its spring water products to druggists and grocers as far away as Montreal, St. Louis, and Philadelphia.

Similar to the merchandizing efforts of the Milford Mineral Springs owners, the Cohas Spring's brochure flaunted the water's superior taste as attributed to "... the rock formation contains but a trace of soluble mineral matter needed to give the waters issuing from it the required zest without any objectionable hardness." Not surprisingly, the brochure goes on to warn the consuming public of the inherent dangers of municipal waters as "...positively dangerous and more of it is unpalatable or even repulsive."

Records are not available to indicate how bottled Cohas Spring water was distributed or what the new company's sales volumes might have been. Some "tonics" were apparently produced by Cohasaqua in keeping with their written corporate charter. A surviving color label for a 15 oz bottle of Cohas Birch Beer displays a Native American image with the description:

> Made from the famous Cohas Spring water, highly carbonated. Combined with the flavoring principles of sweet birch. Sweetened with pure sugar. Manufactured and guaranteed by the Cohasaqua Corporation under the Food and Drug Act, June 30, 1906, U.S. serial number 55633.

At least some of the flavored tonics sold under the Cohas label may not have been physically bottled in the North Londonderry facilities. One reputable beverage history reference source indicates that the D. Daoust Company of Manchester bottled a Cohas Raspberry Soda. Quite possibly the Daoust operators, which bottled a host of other flavored sodas including Ginger Brandy, Special Root Beer, and their Bo-La brand, served as contract bottlers to Cohas Springs during this period.

Illustration 3 The Cohas Spring complex in North Londonderry showing the visitor's center and adjacent bottling plant with the tracks of the Manchester to Derry trolley tracks in the foreground. Credit: ImageAbility.

Success in the spring water business was far from assured as history repeatedly demonstrates. Records reflect a period of inactivity at the North Londonderry site following the business failure of the Cohasaqua Corporation. However, the opportunity for success captured the attention of yet a third group of entrepreneurs, Frederick Brown and Frederick Beckwith of Dover, New Hampshire. They purchased the Cohas spring and associated land and structures in late 1921 and established an operation under the name Brobeco Corporation. These new, enthusiastic owners provided the capital to remodel the existing bottling plant by installing a refrigeration system to cool the spring waters to 34 degrees prior to the addition of carbonation and flavorings. A new automated bottling unit with its capacity of 4,800 bottles per hour was also added to complete the upgrade. Known soda flavors from surviving bottle caps during this period included Birch Beer, Root Beer, Ginger Ale and Strawberry (with the production of additional flavors quite likely).

The newly-organized Brobeco enterprise also attempted to attract more day visitors to the site via the construction of a new access road connecting the grounds with Brown Avenue in the Goffs Falls section of Manchester. On June 12, 1922, newspapers announced a gala open house touting the owners' $45,000 investment in the operation and grounds[14]. But the new business owners were apparently no more successful than the previous operators and corporate dissolution occurred by the first of 1923.

The commercial history of Cohas Springs appears closely tied to the creation of the greater Manchester-Nashua electric street trolley system in the early 1900s. The Manchester to Derry Street Railway trolley line was opened in 1907 and branched from the system's main line at Goff's Falls (on the Merrimack River adjacent to the current Manchester Airport). I then ran to the center of Derry via North Londonderry along Little Cohas Brook. The trolley tracks passed directly in front of the spring water complex's bottling plant, and passengers could depart at a trolley stop to partake of the refreshing spring water and enjoy the well-appointed grounds.

However, the freedom provided by rapidly-growing individual automobile ownership in America during the early 20th century sealed the fate of most electric trolley service. This was certainly true throughout New England, and it eventually included main-line passenger trains as well. The never-profitable Manchester to Derry Street Railway was formally abandoned in August 1926.

The Brobeco Corporation ceased operations several years prior to the trolley line's demise, bringing a final end to any commercial activities at the Cohas spring water site. On August 12, 1932, the Manchester newspapers reported that a devastating fire of unknown origin entirely destroyed the site's empty structures. Today, a walking path along the abandoned trolley right-of-way leads to crumbled building foundations and broken glass—the last remnants of a once-effervescent dream.

* * *

LONDONDERRY LITHIA SPRING

Throughout much of the 18th and 19th centuries, European mineral baths and springs were highly valued for their presumed curative effects. The Western European practices followed the bathing traditions started in ancient Greece and Rome. In Greek mythology certain natural springs were believed to be blessed by the gods and therefore could cure diseases if one drank or bathed in them. The Romans brought this same practice to the territories they conquered, including the complex at Bath, Somerset, England. There, geothermal springs deep in the limestone formations allow heated mineral waters to reach the surface.

One mineral component that received special public attention in the mid 1800s in the United States was the alkali metal lithium (from the Greek *lithos* for "rock" or "stone"). Lithium (Li) is a chemical element with an atomic number of 3 that was first discovered by scientists in 1817. The element is comparatively rare geologically, and the metallic form is unstable in most natural environments. However, mineral compounds containing lithium are found widely dispersed in trace amounts in plants, soils and rocks, and in many surface and groundwaters. The degree to which humans are exposed to this naturally-occurring earth element typically depends on both geographic location (where it can be naturally concentrated) and diet (nuts, seeds and certain grains can have a high lithium content). Most current medical researchers do not consider lithium to be an essential or vital micronutrient for an individual's health or well-being.

Long before this naturally-occurring metal became a modern-day essential material for batteries and electronics, it was valued for its purported health-related benefits. When lithium was discovered to be a component of some natural mineral springs, people began to ascribe a range of curative properties to it, including the treatment of rheumatism, asthma, gout and many other ailments. Lithia Springs, Georgia, was the site of sacred healing springs recognized by the Cherokee Nation. An investor group purchased the springs in the 1880s to begin selling bottled waters, and they also developed a spa hotel complete with "Lithia Vapor Baths." The resort evolved to become a prominent American spa destination, entertaining notables from Mark Twain to the Vanderbilts to Presidents Grover Cleveland, William Howard Taft, William McKinley and Theodore Roosevelt. In 1888 over 3,000 tourists and health-seekers found their way to Lithia Springs, Georgia. Might this Southern success story have caught the attention of entrepreneurs in other geographic locales?

New Hampshire's Londonderry Lithia Spring was first discovered in 1882 by the Avery family while looking for a new source of water for their farm located in the town's southwest corner. The family had this new-found spring tested by a Professor H. Halvorson who reported the "alkakine-chaybeate" (high pH, iron rich) waters contained an astounding 8.62 grains of lithium bicarbonate per gallon. Before long, the Averys were bottling their spring water in 3-gallon clay jugs and selling them locally as health waters.[15]

A group led by a General Charles S. Collins of Nashua bought out the Avery family spring and 30 acres of land in 1886 and then added another 100 acres to protect the quality of the water's source. This business group bottled the Londonderry waters in a three-story bottling plant on Elm Street in downtown Nashua complete with adjacent rail-shipping facilities. Company advertising boldly claimed the waters were "The Strongest Natural Lithia

Water in the World" and contrasted its product with inferior "manufactured waters" (i.e., those where lithium and other mineral salts were purposely added).

Illustration 4 By the 1890s Londonderry Lithia spring water was being bottled in a modern, three-story building in downtown Nashua, claimed to be the largest such plant in the county. Credit: ImageAbility.

Londonderry Lithia Spring Water was offered in still form (non-carbonated, its natural state) or sparkling (carbonated at the Nashua bottling works). The healing waters were offered for sale in a range of container sizes, the most common seem to be attractive green quart or gallon glass bottles with paper labels. Smaller volume bottles were apparently used as well; although these appear to have been less commonly used judging by what modern bottle collectors find in today's antique marketplaces.

The brand's owners fully capitalized on the nation's love affair with healing mineral waters and assured its customers that Londonderry Lithia

Spring Water could cure Gravel (kidney stones), Dyspepsia (stomach issues), Bright's disease (inflammation of the kidney), insomnia, apoplexy, rheumatism, and a host of other ailments. Like other mineral waters and some patent medicines of the day, the Londonderry waters were also touted as a sound alternative to alcoholic beverages. The company even claimed that their spring was long known to Native Americans of the area who traveled from the Merrimack River to the Londonderry spring to "avail themselves of its curative virtues."

Illustration 5 Londonderry Lithia offered the consumer a remedy for a host of ailments, including those caused by "high living." Credit: ImageAbility.

Personal testimonies were a key ingredient to any product's advertising campaign in the 19th and early 20th century. Paid advertisements in newspapers of the time were commonly written and presented to read like objective news articles, but they were in essence testimonials from patrons of the product – some real, some fictitious[16]. A portion of an October 18, 1895 article in the renowned *New York Times* illustrates the tone and delivery of this form of quite-convincing advertising.

> It is, and should be, a source of satisfaction to the doctors that they can suggest a simple and at the same time effective remedy for this most perplexing and almost universal malady. It is also a delight to the patient to be ordered to use such a palatable medicine. This fact explains in part the unparalleled success of the water. The patient will take it faithfully, and after once beginning, being sure to note a relief from the pain in a short time, pursues the treatment with religious zeal.

An 1891 printed booklet Informed that Londonderry Lithia Spring Water was "used at all of the prominent clubs and hotels and sold by leading grocers and druggists throughout the United States." At the time, these claims may have been close to accurate, as the company maintained offices in Boston, New York, Chicago, Baltimore, Buffalo, Washington DC, Detroit, Cincinnati, St. Louis and St. Paul. At the 1892 Chicago World's Fair the Londonderry Lithia Spring Water Company occupied a 150 square foot exhibit space completed with a 15-foot replica of one of their water bottles. The reach and market recognition of this New Hampshire-produced spring water was clearly impressive.

As the year 1900 approached, patent medicines and curative products of all types were coming under increased scrutiny by investigative reporters and government agencies for both their wild claims and, in many cases, their actual harmful contents (see more on patent medicines in Chapter 2). Analytical chemistry had advanced considerably, and the investigators were using this as one of their tools to prove deception and outright fraud. The passage of the 1906 U.S. Pure Food and Drug Act mandated that product labels accurately reflect the product's ingredients, putting at least a damper on most unsubstantiated health and curative claims.

Londonderry's Lithia Spring Water desired to have its products' labeling conform to the 1906 act. At least some facets of the U.S. medical community of the time still held that lithium did provide health benefits to the consumer, even if those benefits might be unprovable. Accordingly, the company chose to continue with its advertising campaigns and associated health claims.

Federal agents were not convinced, and in 1910 the U.S. Department of Agriculture seized over 1,700 bottles of Londonderry Lithia Water on suspicion of fraud. Government chemists[17] determined that this spring water contained only a minuscule amount of natural lithium, (1/1200 of a grain, or about 0.014 ppm). The original Halvorson chemical report of the spring water's lithium content and claims based upon it had been off by a country mile.[18] Had this been an honest error, a failure of inexact 19th century analytical testing, or a purposeful deceit? The federal government firmly believed the latter and the seized "product was condemned and forfeited" for destruction.

However, the company operations and sales apparently continued after this federal seizure as a similar raid was conducted by Massachusetts authorities in 1914. With its reputation seriously tarnished and the public increasingly wary of food and beverage product claims, the Londonderry Lithia Spring Water Company ceased operations in 1920 (or as late as 1923 according to some records).

The Pack Monadnock Lithia Spring in Temple, New Hampshire, met a similar fate to its Londonderry cousin. The Temple operation ran from 1891 to 1911 and was developed by one Sidney Scammon and his uncle, Rodney Killam.[19] Like Londonderry's Lithia Spring, the Temple duo boldly claimed their waters could cure a host of ailments. Tank wagons of spring water were carted down to Greenville and Wilton, New Hampshire, as well as Fitchburg, Massachusetts, to be distributed via rail. The pair was exceedingly successful with their water venture and even opened a recreation and picnic grove in the vicinity of their spring – all free to the townspeople. The good times came to a crashing end in 1911, however, when it was discovered that Scammon and Killam were purchasing lithium salts and adding them to the spring water prior to their shipment to customers.

Ironically, lithium does have a legitimate, modern medical role as it is sometimes used to treat mental disorders, including bipolar conditions, depression and schizophrenia. For many years lithium carbonate was the gold standard for Bipolar Affective Disorder (BPAD) and is still commonly employed today. The element's suitability for treating for other medical conditions, or the purported benefits of taking micro-doses for general wellness purposes, are much less defined and verifications remain controversial.

* * *

THE ENDING OF AN ERA

Several developments beyond poor management or deceitful practices contributed to the demise of most of the localized springs in New Hampshire that bottled and sold their waters commercially. For those enterprises serving the urban market, the growing practice of chlorinating municipal drinking water for the control of bacteria and other microorganisms was a primary factor leading to an increased confidence in the safety of tap water. This institutional treatment effort started successfully in the City of Philadelphia in 1913 and then spread rapidly to other major cities. Tap water had quickly become more dependable and importantly, a more trusted commodity. This was especially true in municipalities that obtained their drinking water from high-quality, protected sources such as local lakes and reservoirs. Those city water works drew from a source that readily garnered the public's confidence. Manchester and Nashua are but two examples of this factor.

> In New Hampshire all bottled spring waters are considered a regulated food product and licensed by the Department of Health and Human Services. Independent inspections and periodic testing for chemical content and purity are required.

Another major reason for the decline in the bottled water market at the beginning of the 20th century was likely the effects of the 1906 Pure Food and Drug Act. While this federal act was primarily targeted at the drug-laced or high-alcohol "patent" medicines, certainly much of the general public had considered spring waters, mineral waters, and certainly spa waters as medicinal agents as well. Now, many of those products were cast in the same dubious light as the bottled snake oils and "miracle" elixir cures.

Outlandish product claims of all types were being exposed as fraud – or at least being examined in the new light of sound medical, chemical and geological sciences. As professional medical care increased in America, the reliance on self-medication through home remedies and patent medicines naturally decreased. All of this had an impact on the commercial sales of mineral waters and spring waters, and many such establishments simply ceased being profitable ventures. Changes in public attitude and acceptance of science over unsubstantiated claims did not happen overnight, of course. As late as 1931, the Poland Spring operation was still issuing pamphlets with titles such as "Mineral Waters Therapeutically Considered" to promote the health benefits of its spring waters. But New Hampshire's first spring water era was largely a closed chapter by the 1920s.

Today, about 55% of New Hampshire residents obtains their drinking water from groundwater sources–either private on-site wells or through municipal water systems that tap into significant aquifers for their supply. Notwithstanding the safety, convenience, and low cost of tap water, we still contract for home-delivered bottled water or purchase shrink-wrapped cases of single-serve bottles from our local supermarkets and big box stores. The practice is pervasive and growing as we'll see in Chapter 6's discussion of bottled waters' "second act."

2   THE GOLDEN AGE OF BOTTLED REMEDIES, ELIXIRS AND TONICS

The knowledge of sound medical science advanced rapidly in the 19th century, but many of these practices did not gain wide-spread acceptance by the consumer public until the early 20th century. The healthcare landscape in New Hampshire throughout the 1800s was not unlike that found in the rest of the other forty-four states and territories. Midwives, local druggists, physicians and medicine men of various qualifications all prescribed remedies for those in need of curing or even those thinking they had an ailment or "condition" requiring treatment.

In the still-developing United States of 1800, there were only four true medical schools to receive any formal training: Boston's Harvard College,

New Hampshire's Dartmouth College, Columbia in New York and the College of Philadelphia (later the University of Pennsylvania). Diplomas were issued for two years of study and many physicians learned their trade primarily by serving as an apprentice to individuals who were also poorly trained. Those wishing more thorough medical training typically sought that from Europe: London, Edinburgh or Paris – assuming they could afford such an education in the first place.

With the rapidly mushrooming American population, the typical local physician of this time was not necessarily a qualified, board-certified practitioner; and many "doctors" simply adopted that title because it benefited them and their enterprise. As late as 1870 the head of the Harvard Medical School reported that written examinations could not be given to medical students because not enough of them could write well enough. Some would say that ailing patients probably had a better chance of recovery by NOT seeing their local physician.

Thus, it probably shouldn't be surprising that many 19th century Americans either had a distrust of the medical profession, such that it was, or simply couldn't afford to pay for such services. Home remedies, the neighborhood herbalist, and even those hawking cure-alls in a bottle all found themselves serving a niche with the working population.

This was certainly nothing new, since in the 1700s both the Englishman and the American of all classes and social standing were well accustomed to availing themselves of a wide array of self-prescribed medications. In his first voyage to New England in 1602, British explorer Bartholomew Gosnold's crew harvested sassafras tree bark and pith to bring back to their homeland for processing[20]. As it grew and developed, Colonial America quite customarily drew from readily-available English remedies and medicines, at least up to the Revolutionary War period. By necessity during the war years, the rebellious Colonists started to develop their own medicines for commercial sale.

The Colonial Americans could rightly claim an established tradition of using botanical medicines because early European settlers learned from Native Americans who well-understood the medicinal value of plants and herbs. For example, prior to the invention of aspirin in 1897, there was nothing to alleviate pain besides plant medicines. Willow bark and meadowsweet were known to the Native Americans and offered some form of mild relief. This natural connection partially explains the prevalent use of Native American images and symbols throughout the patent medicine era — a practice that continued with the marketing of mineral waters and carbonated beverages.

After the Revolutionary War ended, the shipment of British medicines and other goods resumed, but the embryonic domestic industry was already well on its way to its own form of made-in-America independence. The U.S. patent medicine business began to organize and thrive as the year 1800 approached. From about 100 different nostrums available in 1810, the American public enjoyed a selection of over 50,000 remedies by 1906, mostly liquids that were sold in glass bottles[21]. Those products represented sales of $80 million – over $2 billion in today's dollars.

Not all medicines were patented; in fact, few were. Applying for patents took time, money, and gave away the owner's "secret formula." Many remedies of the 19th century were simply registered to protect the product trade name. These were more correctly *proprietary medicines* as such, but the term *patent medicine* is commonly applied generically to all types of medicines sold without a prescription. Elixirs, remedies, nostrums, and tonics all fit into this generic term for practical purposes and are therefore used interchangeably in this chapter.

* * *

THE NEW HAMPSHIRE EXPERIENCE

The first business directory for Manchester, New Hampshire, was published in 1844 and reflected three druggists operating in the city. Ten years later there were five times that number, and between 1890 and 1900 over 80 apothecaries and medicine manufacturers operated in the City of Manchester alone[22]. The sales of patent medicines were substantial, and stock included products that were marketed nationally and internationally as well as local offerings. In the 1890s Manchester druggist F.H. Thurston carried seventeen brands of locally-produced bitters in addition to the nationally-distributed ones.

In the era before Big Pharma and Big Government, local druggists and physicians commonly concocted and sold their own versions of popular remedies. In addition to the famous Dr. Kilmer's Swamp Root and Hood's Sarsaparilla, New Hampshire folks could purchase Preston's Vegetable Catholicon (Portsmouth), Dr. Copp's White Mountain Anti-Bilious Bitters (Manchester), or Goffstown's own Indian Pile Remedy.

Shortly after the end of the Civil War, Wilton entrepreneur Philander Ring entered into a partnership with two other gentlemen, a Peterborough chemist and a future New Hampshire Governor and U.S. Senator[23]. They formed a company selling bottles of Ring's Vegetable Ambrosia for Gray Hair and later (without the involvement of the future Governor), Ring's Witch Hazel Ointment – the "Greatest Healer on Earth."

Figure 2 Representative of the myriad of available products, this Manchester druggist offered Essence of Checkerberry (wintergreen extract).

A Dover pharmacist, H. C. Goodwin, offered his clientele his formulations of Compound Syrup of Sarsaparilla and Dr. Lewis' Cholera Cordial, "a certain and safe remedy for cholera morbus, dysentery, and diarrhea or summer complaints…" Gastrointestinal ailments were of course as common to New Hampshirites as they were to fellow countrymen, and especially during the hot summer months when untreated water supplies and unrefrigerated foods were susceptible to bacterial outbreaks.

While pamphlets, hand bills, colorful trade cards and even painted farmers' barns were all common venues for advertising one's latest cure-all, newspapers were the undisputed media-of-choice of the times. Throughout the 1800's newspapers derived a substantial income from running advertisements for patent medicines and other medical-related products. Many of these placements were straight forward space ads, such as H.F. Thayer's Mme. Augusta Healy's Vegetable Tonic Pills. But as often, the pitch for a particular product was thinly disguised as a brief news article heralding a scientific or medical breakthrough and "It only costs a dollar!"

Herbal remedies of various types were offered by the country's Shaker communities, with many already experiencing a thriving commercial packaged seed business. This included the New Hampshire communities at Canterbury Village and Enfield. The Shakers' good name was well recognized in broad society as a synonym for reputable, well-made merchandise backed by an industrious and honest group of workers. As a result, the herbal medicinal products market was well suited for their communal endeavors and savvy business focus[24].

Shakers throughout all the communities prepared and sold at least two hundred different botanicals, some as dried material in tins, some as bricks, and some as prepared liquid remedies. So-called Shaker Anodyne, or Brown's Pure Extract of English Valerian, was made and sold by the Enfield community. Reportedly it costs the Shakers $2.25 to make a dozen bottles and they sold those to distributors for $6.00. The distributors then marked up the product 50% for sale to the public ($0.75 a bottle), a fairly standard mark-up for patent medicines of the day.[25]

> The average patent medicine and nostrum dealer was able to create a lucrative business for themselves if they had an effective advertising campaign that could instill in people's minds that even minor aches and pains need not be ignored. The illustrated trade card was an integral part of any such advertising campaign.
> Source: Ferraro and Ferraro, 1964.

The Enfield Shaker community also supplied some of the country's larger commercial manufacturers of medicinals, including the giant Lowell, Massachusetts enterprises of Charles I. Hood and John C. Ayer. As an example, records indicate that in 1889 the Enfield community shipped some forty-four thousand pounds of yellow dock to the Ayer Company for use in their famous sarsaparilla compound[26]. That shipment was valued at the tidy sum of $22,000, demonstrating just how financially attractive the patent medicine business was at the time.

A Shaker brother at the Canterbury community, Dr. Thomas J. Corbett, was well-known for his knowledge of botanical medicines and their curative properties. He was a follower of New Hampshire native Samuel Thomson, a self-taught but highly recognized herbalists and botanist who was born in Alstead in 1769. Thomson would practice in Surry and surrounding towns, becoming the acknowledged founder of the widely-influential alternative system of medicine known as "Thomsonian Medicine."

Starting in 1835, Brother Corbett developed at least four products for the Canterbury community to sell to the public: Corbett's Dyspepsia Cure (a laxative), Corbett's Shaker Wild Cherry Pectoral Syrup (for coughs), Vegetable Family Pills, and most notably, Corbett's Syrup of Sarsaparilla. This last item, created in 1843, was produced continuously up until at least 1910 and was one of the few Shaker products to be truly patented.

Unlike other merchants of patent medicines, the honest Shakers did not claim "secret formulas," and their literature informed the consumer that the Corbett remedy was a mixture of sarsaparilla roots, dandelion, yellow dock, mandrake, black cohosh, garget, Indian hemp, the berries of juniper and cubeb, and iodine of potassium. These ingredients were selected "… because we know them to be the best in the vegetable kingdom, and because we carefully select every one according to its power." Some Shaker literature actually provided recipes and instructions for preparing their remedies–quite in contrast to the less-forthright sellers of the vast majority of patent medicines in the 19th century.

As with almost all patent medicines, advertising almost always included testimonials from cured patients, satisfied parents, and members of the medical profession. Mary Whitcher, a leading figure of the Canterbury Shaker community, produced a *Shaker House-Keeper* handbook in 1882, which listed some 20 druggists from around New Hampshire who vouched for the value of the Corbett's Shaker Syrup of Sarsaparilla and also included an abundance of testimonials from individuals as well[27].

By the last quarter of the 19th century, sales of New Hampshire Shaker medicine products were dwindling and the variety of offerings greatly reduced. This was a reflection of competition from the abundantly-available and efficiently-produced outside products coupled with the steady decline of available workers within the Enfield and Canterbury Shaker communities[28]. The manufacture of the Sarsaparilla Syrup, for instance, was an especially labor-intensive and time-consuming process requiring the use of several buildings followed by a three-month aging step before packaging and labeling. In 1914 the Canterbury community contracted to sell their syrup to the Walsh and Cummings Pharmacy in Manchester, accepting a portion of the product's profit in return. By 1919, however, the production of Sarsaparilla Syrup ceased altogether[29]. An era had ended.

> **Shaker Tincture of Skunk Cabbage (1883)**
> 3 oz. skunk cabbage root
> 1 qt. spirits
> Stand 1 week
> Dose: teasp-Table
> Use: Asthma, hysteria
> Source: Hall, 2007.

Significantly, most all pre-1900 patent medicines were plant-based, having preceded the development of chemical and bio-chemical based products, which came about in the early 20th century. Ardent botanical practitioners and supporters like to point to two notable early discoveries—

quinine, the alkaloid extracted from cinchona bark used for the treatment of malaria, and digitalis, derived from the foxglove plant, used for certain heart diseases.

However, by the latter half of the 19th century many of the commercially-available remedies on the market had come to contain directly harmful substances such as chloroform, morphine, cocaine and most commonly, alcohol. Such substances could be highly addictive and pose a definable and tangible risk to a healthy life. Early detractors and reformist-minded investigators of the day claimed that more alcohol was sold via patent medicines than was sold through licensed liquor sales[30].

The 1866 herbal compendium by Dr. O. Phelps Brown presented the public with recipes for hundreds of medications, both topical and for ingestion, for just about anything that ailed them or their families. The message of Brown's *The Complete Herbalist, or the People Their Own Physicians* couldn't be more direct: the curative powers you seek are to be found right within the pages of this tome. Just two examples of Brown's alcohol-based formulas illustrate their composition:

SARSAPARILLA SYRUP

No. 9. Good sarsaparilla, two pounds; guaiacum, three ounces; rose leaves, two ounces; senna, two ounces; liquorice root, two ounces; oil of sassafras, five drops; oil of aniseed, five drops; oil of wintergreen, three drops; diluted alcohol, ten pints; sugar, eight pounds.

Dose – One table spoonful two or three times a day.

STOMACH BITTERS

No. 14. Gentian root, two ounces; dried orange peel, one ounce; cardamom seed, half an ounce (all bruised); diluted alcohol or common whiskey, one quart. Let it stand for two weeks.

Use – Dyspepsia, loss of appetite, general weakness, etc.
Dose – One or two table spoonsful in water three times a day.

Could these two remedies be used by the consumer as directed without serious detriment and possibly with some actual beneficial effects on the patient's symptoms? The answer would have to be a qualified "yes." Minus the alcohol, the Sarsaparilla Syrup recipe is very close to many common root beer soda recipes, even those used today. For the Stomach Bitters, gentian root has known digestive benefits and remains an ingredient in Moxie soda, a brand currently owned and distributed by Coca-Cola into grocery and convenient stores throughout the Northeast states.

Sounding close to a patented cure-all, Concord, New Hampshire's own Berry's Famous Root Beer advertised in the summer of 1902 that it could prevent sunstroke because it "Acts on the blood, cools and purifies it, and cures thirst." Of course, the simple point to be made here is that even the patent medicines or beverages that "only" contained alcohol (as opposed to agents such as cocaine), could be misrepresented, misused and abused.

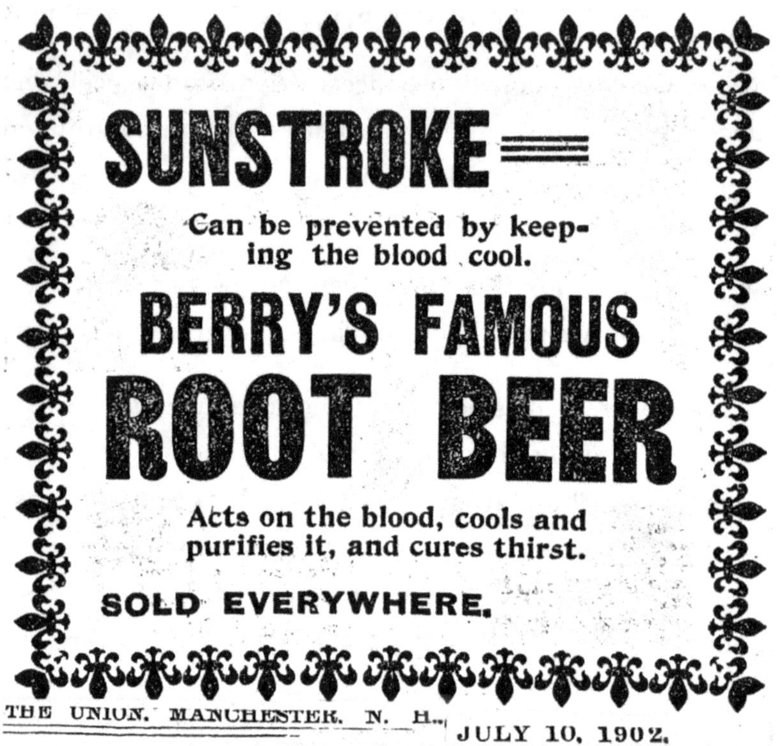

Illustration 6 This 1902 newspaper ad reflects the era surrounding the passage of the 1906 Food and Drug Act when merchants were toning down health claims, but not eliminating them entirely.

Not much changed in the patent medicine industry until a host of investigative reports were published after the turn of the century. The most prominent and influential of these was an 11-part series run in the *Collier's Weekly* in 1905-1906 entitled "The Great American Fraud" by investigative reporter Samuel Hopkins Adams. The passage of the federal 1906 Pure Food and Drug Act was a watershed event, but industry reform did not exactly come about immediately. This is not surprising given the significant financial gains to be had within the patent medicine industry–both by the commercial giants as well as the smaller local or regional merchants.

In 1907 a New York State report listed the alcohol content of many of the popular liquid patent medicines sold to the public. Some products tested contained as much as 35 percent alcohol. Famed and respected Ayer's Sarsaparilla contained 26.2 percent alcohol and the equally esteemed Lowell product, Hood's Sarsaparilla, some 18.8 percent. Even Corbett's Shaker Sarsaparilla was found to contain 8.8 percent alcohol by volume. But these products were the everyday vehicles of treatment for medical conditions and pain relief experienced by American citizens of all stripes and classes, even those from "respectable" 19th century society.

Figure 3 Thurston's Drug Store, Manchester ca. 1900 was typical of a thriving and well-stocked pharmacy of that era. Credit: Manchester Historic Association.

The growing realization of both the harm many of these unregulated agents were causing, coupled with the rampant unsubstantiated product benefit claims, directly led to the passage of the 1906 Pure Food and Drug Act.

The Act did not outright ban most patent medicines, but it severely restricted the maker's false claims and certainly targeted the misleading advertising and labeling. In the Granite State the Act's passage warranted only a brief article in the *Manchester Union* newspaper, but the effect on advertising began to become more evident even in that same year. Ad claims became less extravagant, and many companies experiencing decreased sales curtailed their advertising budgets or ceased altogether. In 1905 twelve drug manufacturers were listed in Manchester's city directory; by 1908 there were only four.[31]

The 1906 Act clearly represented a pivotal point in the American food, beverage and medications industries, effecting how products could be presented and marketed. This all resulted in the public's growing understanding of sound health science and their wariness concerning the safety and efficacy of most unregulated patent medicines. Increasingly, governmental agencies coupled with the maturing medical profession were looked upon as the authorities who had the public's well-being in mind; this was not the case with the itinerant nostrum salesman, or even the home-concocted tonics of one's parents or grandparents.

> Fermented ginger beer, popular in the early 1800; was made from sugar, citrus juices, honey, ginger, and water.
> Source: Riley, 1972.

We've seen that as the 19th century came to a close the patent medicine marketplace was facing major pressures, and significant changes were in the works. An equally strong movement paralleled those social and medical concerns over unregulated drugs—the American temperance movement. Starting in the 1820s and building widespread support, by the turn of the century temperance societies were commonplace in communities across the United States. Alcohol was viewed as a destabilizing and destructive force toward marriages and family units, especially by women. A renewed wave of activism began in 1906 and culminated with a period of National Prohibition starting in 1920 and extending until 1933.

Many herb or root-based products with at least some substantiated health or well-being benefits altered their formulas to remove banned or suspected harmful ingredients. With moderated advertising claims, they could continue to offer their product to a willing portion of the American public. One New Hampshire company that seem to thrive in this manner was Thall's Home Remedies Laboratory of Manchester. Almost nothing is known regarding the training or background of the company's founder and chief chemist, David S. Thall. While his enterprise was routinely listed in Manchester City Directories and the New Hampshire Register over a period of several decades, and obtained a federal trademark in 1928 and again in 1947, it appears that he may have never registered with the State of New Hampshire as a formal business concern.

> In 1940 the per capita annual consumption of carbonated sodas in the U.S. reached the 100-drink mark.
> Source: Riley, 1972.

Nevertheless, Thall's practice was first recognized in the 1925 Manchester City Directory under "medicines" and by 1931 was listed as Thall's Home Remedies. Thall operated at various city locations including 416 Beech Street, and for a twenty-year period, in the active business section of Manchester Street just off of the main thoroughfare of Elm Street. A company brochure of the era shows a bustling store front at 82 Manchester Street and a photo of a distinguished-looking David Thall, "proprietor and manufacturer," wearing a white lab coat or pharmacist's smock. Another brochure contains short testimonials by satisfied users.

One of Thall's brochures from 1936[32] lists some 20 specific compounds, ointments, powders, liniments or drops that customers could purchase to further their health and wellbeing. Offerings included:

> Thall's No. 30 Compound – Iron Tonic – "Useful as a tonic and to improve the blood."
>
> Thall's No. 5 Ointment – "Useful to relieve rheumatic affections, colds, stiffness, swelling, and sprains."
>
> Thall's Liberty Corn Salve – "Useful for corns, callouses, and warts."
>
> Thall's Toothache Drops – "For toothaches."

Most of the listed products sold at a price between 25 cents and a dollar and guaranteed that:

> All the Thall's Home Remedies are absolutely pure and contain no harmful ingredients. A pleasant tasting and affective, non-narcotic and non-alcoholic. They are well preserved for a long stand.

These product claims contained in company brochures were likely toned-down versions of earlier advertising, since in 1933 Thall was charged under the federal Food and Drug Act for "adulteration and misbranding" of a number of his remedies. He subsequently paid a $425 fine to the U.S. Department of Agriculture. However, Thall's Home Remedies Laboratory apparently operated well into the 1960s.

* * *

MINERAL WATERS AS MEDICINE? WHAT DID SCIENCE SAY?

What about mineral waters as therapeutic or curative agents? Certainly, as we saw in the preceding chapter, many 18th and 19th century Americans viewed spring waters and mineral waters as beneficial agents – sort of nature-provided elixirs. By the second half of the 19th century, the bottling of water was a well-established American industry with such vibrancy that, in an interesting economic turnabout, some of our bottled waters were actually exported back into Europe.

The thriving bottled water industry of this time provided consuming citizens with the expectation of purchasing a worthwhile product that would deliver them healthy outcomes. But could the water purveyors deliver on such a promise?

> The inconclusiveness and sporadic nature of [water quality] tests, combined with physicians' egos (not to mention their need for funds), often resulted in confused, contradictory, and sometimes dangerous prescriptions of mineral waters.[33]

At the well-known Saratoga Springs in New York, the diverse chemical composition of many of the springs led to a complex medical program to attempt to use the waters effectively.

> The waters are a cathartic, alterative, diuretic, and tonic. Each spring has the salts and solutions in different proportions which gives it a peculiar virtue and adapts it more particularly to certain forms of disease. Columbia Spring is a fine chalybeate (iron-bearing) tonic, gives tone and strength to the stomach, improves the condition of the blood by increasing the number of red corpuscles. It is useful in all

diseases characterized by impoverished condition of the blood. Dose: From half a glass to one glass before meals; its use is better preceded by cathartic water. Hawthorne Spring as a cathartic is unrivaled in potency by any spring in Saratoga, and in this its danger lies. It is highly beneficial in dyspepsia, chronic constipation, gout, rheumatism, and in liver and kidney difficulties.[34]

Such sweeping "guidance" couldn't help but beg the question:

So, were mineral waters healthy or dangerous? It depended upon who you asked, which spring you referred to, how much water you consumed, under whose guidance you did so, and for what purpose. Such ambiguity both helped and harmed physicians' efforts at convincing citizens to imbibe mineral waters.[35]

A scientific-sounding term was even developed in the late 19th century to described the therapeutic uses of water: "medical hydrology." This concept of melding medical benefits with the study of natural surface and groundwaters carried into the early 20th century through established medical societies, national symposia, and published journals.[36] Thermal springs even played a major role in the development of many of our Nations Parks, such as Hot Springs, Arkansas, and Yellowstone. And while no New England natural springs came close to rivaling the national recognition and extensive fan base of the well-established Saratoga Springs (Maine's Poland Spring came closest), even the most primitive New Hampshire springs tried to mimic the country's successful sites.

While a fair portion of medical hydrology concerned itself with water as a physical agent (the beneficial effects of bathing in mineral waters, thermal or otherwise), commercialization of therapeutic waters required legitimate chemical analyses of the waters' composition. Scientists developed legitimate classification protocols to categorize waters based their major dissolved constituents, namely minerals and gases. In effect, they were trying to bring the next level of objective evidence to what previously largely unsubstantiated claims of water quality and associated health benefits. If water was to be prescribed and ingested for its healing properties, then precise and reliable chemical analyses were a must.

> In the early 19th century, ginger was viewed as highly therapeutic and therefore a natural component to any beverage that aspired to also provide the consumer with health benefits. Ginger's recognized benefits have been carried forward to modern times.
> Source: Witzel and Young-Witzel, 1998.

To satisfy this need for credible analytical data, improved techniques for the field and laboratory were developed by both governmental and private sector chemists ("geochemists" really). In addition to the major mineral components, analytical testing was developed for trace elements in waters–lithium, regarded as a useful treatment for kidney stones, and arsenic, which was believed to hold therapeutic value in the treatment of some skin diseases, the gastrointestinal trace, and other organs.

Who knew that 1876 would turn out to be a watershed year in American science and medicine? That year the first academic institution in the United States was established primarily for graduate studies: Johns Hopkins University of Baltimore. The Johns Hopkins Hospital, thoroughly modern in both design and patient care systems, opened in 1889 with the University School of Medicine following just four years later. The graduating physicians of the University were to become the front-line medical leaders of America,

Old Yankees would say that a man never wanted to marry a "Lydia Pinkham" — code language for a constantly complaining woman!
Source: Farrow, 1985.

applying sound science to the practice of medicine and helping to sunset the older folk-based medical treatments.

The widespread therapeutic use of spring and mineral waters did not disappear overnight, of course, but a new era was clearly dawning in late 19th century America. Granted, these medicinal waters (and the botanical tonics) had provided a welcomed, safer alternative to many of the harsh and harmful patent medicines—the ones laced with cocaine, alcohol, or mercury. It would take strong action starting with the passage of the 1906 Food and Drug Act to dispel the more dangerous demons lurking in the overabundance of patent medicines available to the unwitting public. But a well-trained, science-based physician corps would prove to be the vanguard of permanent change, and Johns Hopkins and other institutions that followed their lead were instrumental in bringing this sweeping change to the American public.

* * *

THE NEXT CHAPTER

Today's consumer can still readily purchase health and wellness-related products such as Hyland's Nerve Tonic for stress relief or Lydia Pinkham's Herbal Supplement with black cohosh and dandelion root (no longer owned or controlled by the Pinkham family). Of course, the supermarket or health food store shopper is also free to select from an almost endless choice of off-the-shelf herbal teas, extracts, tinctures and health supplements.

In this new era, the common saying "as one door closes, another opens" aptly applies to at least one category of food and beverage – carbonated soft drinks. In the next chapter we'll see the rise in fortunes of the drug store soda fountain and the advent of the bottling, marketing and consumption of fizzy drinks for pure refreshment. Both would grow to become powerful economic engines in their own right, as well as recognized American cultural phenomena. Then, following the long reign of fizzy drinks, spring waters and mineral waters would stage their triumphant comeback.

3 THE ADVENT OF THE SODA FOUNTAIN AND BOTTLED SOFT BEVERAGES

REFRESHMENT AT THE AMERICAN DRUG STORE

Well into the 20th century America drug stores remained locally owned, relatively small establishments. In addition to the wide array of medical concoctions and remedies discussed in the previous chapter, drug stores of the period commonly sold other wares and might also offer a range of services to bring customers into the store. Public telephone booths were a logical addition to the corner pharmacy in an era when few households owned a private telephone. In later years vacuum tube testing machines would draw in the do-it-yourselfer trying valiantly to be the home hero by getting the family's radio or television set in working order again. But by far the largest attraction and money-maker for most drug stores was an American-refined European import–the neighborhood soda fountain.

The Advent of the Soda Fountain and Bottled Soft Beverages

The early drug store soda fountain was a natural extension of the pharmacist's medicine and remedy trade. Many patent medicines of the 1800s were formulated specifically for single dose applications as either general pain relievers or to attack specific maladies such as dyspepsia and stomach discomfort, coughs and respiratory afflictions, tiredness due to blood deficiencies, or the dreaded "loss of manhood." Who better to respond than the local druggist-chemist with their ability to quickly access a vast inventory of compounds and administer a needed on-the-spot remedy? Eager patrons willingly pushed their coins across the pharmacy's countertop as the welcomed relief-in-a-glass was delivered in their direction by an obliging neighborhood professional.

The public of the early 1800s already understood that the earth's mineral waters could have health benefits, and the ones containing natural carbonation imparted an extra experience–pleasantly so. The bubbles of carbonation have a decidedly refreshing taste and mouth sensation appealing to the human palette. Around the time of the American Revolution here in the Colonies, English scientist Joseph Priestly and Swedish chemistry professor Torbern Bergman invented methods for infusing water with carbon dioxide. Priestley had discovered what he termed "fixed air" by going to a brewery and collection carbon dioxide coming off the fermenting beer. When he then bubbled the collected gas through a vessel of water some of the gas dissolved giving the water a slight "tang," not unlike many natural spa waters. Priestley had in fact created a carbonated beverage in 1772, not really dissimilar to our modern-day club soda[37].

J.J. Schweppe founded his famous Schweppes Company in Geneva in 1783 by capitalizing on these earlier inventions and moving them out of the research laboratories. The commercial fizzy water market was born. Within the next decade, Schweppe moved his operations to London with the aim of serving an even larger base of consumers. Interestingly, the British government considered Schweppe's fizzy water a medicine, not a refreshment beverage, and accordingly slapped a medical tax on it.

Others improved on the early carbonation techniques, and in 1807 British inventor Henry Thompson was granted a patent for making "soda water." (Even though there was no soda involved – sodium carbonate or bicarbonate). However, sparkling waters quickly assumed this identifier by the general public. Yale chemistry professor Benjamin Silliman garners the credit for bringing European equipment to New Haven, Connecticut, in 1806 to start a soda water business. Unlike Schweppe's refreshment business model, Silliman's intended purpose was to sell a medicinal product. His early advertising claimed that his soda water would cure sour stomachs, heartburn, poor appetites and headaches. The Yale professor's early success and subsequent expansion to New York City and Baltimore demonstrated the potential of the American market and others followed his lead.

> Flavoring natural waters with sarsaparilla, ginger, or even birch or spruce was not only done to create a pleasurable beverage, but was often a way of disguising the taste of an inferior drinking water supply.
> Source: Witzel and Young-Witzel, 1998.

Entrepreneurs John Matthews and John Lippincott began manufacturing an improved carbonation device in the United States in 1832. In the process of getting established, Matthews actually bought out the first female patent holder in the soda water business, Sophia Usher, the widow of an early mineral water maker from New York. Other similar-minded entrepreneurs would soon follow Matthews and Lippincott, most notably Boston's Alvin D. Puffer and James W. Tufts.

The change from offering plain mineral waters to an effervescent flavored and sweetened drink was well underway by the 1830s. Fruit juices were understandably the early choices for flavor additives. The 1833 *Dispensatory of the United States of America* presents recipes for making syrups from mulberries, strawberries, raspberries and pineapples "...to flavor drinks and are much used as grateful additions to carbonic acid waters." In the days before refrigeration, keeping fruit juice flavoring fresh was clearly a challenge, and spoilage was common.

Enter the Tilden & Company of New Lebanon, New York, one of the first true pharmaceutic manufactures in the New World who learned herbal growing and preparation techniques from their local Shaker community. In the 1840s and 1850s the Tilden family developed an extensive business of creating medicinal extracts from herbs and other botanicals selling directly to physicians. They pioneered the use of alcohol to extract the essential constituents from roots and herbs, including sarsaparilla.

> In 1871, the first U.S. trademark for a carbonated drink was awarded to Lemon's Superior Sparkling Ginger Ale of Hartford, Connecticut. There was no lemon flavoring in the recipe – William Lemon was one of the bottling company's three company founders.
> Source: Riley, 1972.

An 1856 advertisement proudly declared, "This establishment is the only one in the country where medicinal extracts of all kinds are prepared *in vaco* (under vacuum) from foreign and indigenous plants."[38]

While the Tildens were solely interested in the medical applications of such extractive processes, it did not take other innovators long to recognize that a means for creating stable flavorings had also been achieved. By the 1860s pharmacists could offer their patrons a wealth of flavored soda waters, some with medicinal or health implications, others just for the pleasure of a refreshing drink. Since some druggists were also capable chemists, many of them started small laboratories to create artificial flavors and colors for their beverage concoctions. Synthetic vanilla flavoring became the key taste ingredient for all "cream" sodas, for instance. Many of these artificial flavorings were colorless, and druggists learned to add dyes to their mix to mimic the natural colors of fruits and juices. Red for cherry or strawberry, green for lemon-lime, etc. Burnt sugar yielded caramel which imparted both a taste and a brown color to soda waters–and is still used today in virtually all colas.

Pharmacists experimented widely and wildly to create something unique enough to attract loyal paying patrons. Blood orange, crabapple, kola champaign, and walnut cream were but a fraction of the offerings that could be enjoyed by the post-Civil War public. One source indicates that by 1877 New York City residents were quenching their thirst by consuming some 200,000 glasses of flavored soda water a day, individually prepared by their friendly druggists. Proprietors were indeed doing quite well with their bubbly liquid offerings, and some went even further with experimental blends that included milk and eventually, of course, ice cream. With made-on-the-spot refreshing beverages gaining rapidly in popularity, the soda fountain equipment became more and more elaborate, both technically and stylistically. Many of the available models even resembled ornate temples to refreshment that helped entice the paying public.

It was Gustavus D. Dows just across the New Hampshire border in Lowell, Massachusetts that can be considered the father of the American soda fountain as we know it. In the 1850s Dows experimented with carbonation equipment for his Lowell pharmacy and introduced his soda fountain in 1858, patenting it in 1861. Made of polished marble with ornate handles and faucets, Dows' soda fountain[39] ushered in an era of design elegance for the humble corner drug store. The self-contained fountain for creating "ice cream sodas" included cooling coils, containers for holding flavored syrups and cream, and an ice shaver, all for the tidy sum of $225 (over $8,000 in 2023 currency). The soda fountain was a central fixture and work of art launched in Lowell that was to be widely copied, as its popularity continued to grow rapidly in the second half of the 1800s.[40]

New Hampshire's pharmacies did their part in keeping up with the stylish upgrades of the larger establishments in Boston, New York and Philadelphia. This from the *Portsmouth Herald* on June 10, 1898:

> Benjamin Green, the druggist, opened his elegant new store at No. 1 Market square this morning, and all day long a constant stream of customers and visitors have filed the palace-like place of business to admire this richly fitted pharmacy.
>
> The store contains an onyx soda fountain of magnificent tile like construction with the most improved system of syrup tanks and taps, entirely original, handsome mirrors and in every way the most artistic and complete that it is possible to conceive.
>
> In every way possible the place is fitted grandly and made to handsomely meet the demands of the increasing business that made the removal from the old store necessary.

It is certainly possible that Benjamin Green's pharmacy owned a copy of *The Standard Manual of Soda and Other Beverages, A Treatise Especially Adapted to the Requirements of Druggists and Confectioners,* published just the previous year. Among this guidebook's 1,500 formulas could be found recipes for mineral waters and salts, medicinal drinks, refreshment drinks, and even sage advice on how best to promote and advertise soda offerings. Print advertisements in the back of the treatise offered druggists a wide array of soda fountain supplies such as counter stools, cup holders, spoons and ladles, and of course beverage syrups and flavorings.

The Standard Manual also offered druggist and other proprietors advice on how to advertise their products and services to the public. "The soda fountain offers opportunities for successful advertising not presented by any other department of a drug store," the guide encouraged. It also assured, "Soda water is now as nearly an article of common consumption as anything not classed as one of the *staffs of life*." The advertising chapter proceeded to coach the proprietor concerning the use of window signs, circulars, newspaper ads, Grand Opening events, and sign boards. In this last category, the sound advice for appealing to passing cyclists is straight-forward, "Wheelmen do not care so much for sweet, foaming drinks, but rather for 'solid,' substantial beverages: kola and coca drinks are favorites with them, owning to their tonic, bracing properties."

There must have been a lot of manly wheelmen-types around New Hampshire in the 1890s because the June 21, 1899 *Portsmouth Herald* reported:

> The ordinary syrups of the soda fountain are taking a back seat, this summer, "said a pharmacy clerk." The honors between moxie (sic) and root beer are about even, though the latter has taken part of the former's sale, … then (followed by) orangeade and coco cola (sic). The sweet drinks seem to be taking a back seat.

Clearly, there was a recognized need to keep those hearty wheelmen of the times hydrated and "braced."

On Manchester's West Side, the mercantile-rich Granite Square was solidly positioned on several street trolley routes providing for an abundance of patrons that passed by the business establishments. Shoppers and those just passing through couldn't help but notice the large sign of W.B. Mitchell's Apothecary proudly advertising "Mitchell's Famous Cream Soda Five Cents."

Figure 4 "Every train stops at Rockingham Junction." With the station structure virtually sitting on the Newfields-Newmarket town line, it well-served the Boston & Maine and Portsmouth & Concord railroads. In the early 1900s this busy crossroads offered waiting passengers such travelers' aides as Preston's Pharmacy (Portsmouth) smelling salts, as well as quick meals and refreshments. Thirsty patrons could enjoy domestic or imported ginger ales, egg phosphates, soda lemonade (i.e., carbonated), Londonderry Lithia Water, or, of course, Moxie.

The soda fountain and its associated offerings had become a substantial American business by the last decade of the century with at least 50,000 such establishments documented by 1895. Many of the ornate fountain devices that ruled court in the larger, urban establishments were modeled after elaborate showcases exhibited at various World's Fairs. As the new century dawned, these garish monuments to refreshment gave way to smaller, sleeker counters with equipment tucked underneath and out of the customer's sight. Improvements in fountain equipment meant that store proprietors no longer needed to be a combination chemist-engineer to operate a soda fountain. Even the necessary carbon dioxide gas could be delivered in pressurized bottles instead of having to be generated in the store's basement "machine works."[41]

Figure 5 The soda fountain of the Walsh & Cummings Pharmacy in Manchester ca. 1932. Note the Moxie display at the far end of the counter. In 1914 this venerable city institution partnered with the Canterbury Shakers to sell the Society's Sarsaparilla Syrup. Credit: The Moxie collection at the Matthews Museum of Maine Heritage.

As popular as drug store fountains were, they could not satisfy every need, everywhere, every time. Most were located in cities or town centers and could be quite removed from the rural populations. Even if you did live down the street from a neighborhood fountain, how could you quench your thirst for a strawberry soda during the late evenings, or on Sundays when the druggist might be closed? Why, bottled beverages were the answer, naturally!

* * *

BOTTLED REFRESHMENT

The bottling of beverages was nothing new of course–mineral waters and beers were first bottled and sold commercially in vessels such as earthenware jugs. The containing of still waters was no more challenging than bottling liquid patent medicines–a hand-blown glass bottle with a simple cork was all that was required. But when mineral waters were artificially carbonated and when early ginger ales and root beers were attempted, the bottling results were often problematic. Carbonation chemist Benjamin Silliman faced this issue in the early 1800s with exploding crockery procured from a New Haven, CT, pottery factory. The container problem would not be fully solved on a mass-commercial basis until nearly 100 years later.

The term *soda pop* appears to have been coined by about 1861 with "pop" referring the sound of a cork or stopper releasing CO_2 from a pressurized bottle upon opening.[42] But keeping that precious CO_2 in a bottle until the desired consumption was akin to wrestling with the proverbial genie. Not surprisingly, the issues came down to basics: the bottles themselves and the closure mechanisms. Throughout the 1800s bottlers and inventors tried to patent over 1,500 types of stoppers and closures for hundreds of different types of beverage bottles.[43]

> In Boston in 1869 bottled lemon soda and sarsaparilla were especially popular.
> Source: Riley, 1972.

The process for making glass bottles was simple but labor-consuming throughout virtually all of the 19th century. Bottles were blown by a skilled individual into a wooden mold (or sometimes iron). Plates with a company or individual proprietor's name and even address could be inserted into the molds prior to the addition of the molten glass. Thus "branded" bottles with specific identifiers could be created fairly easily. Not so easy was the subsequent step to add and shape the bottle's neck and lip by hand-forming a separate piece of molten glass. A reasonable amount of skill was required to get bottle after bottle with finished openings of fairly uniform size. Bottles created with a wide variance in opening diameters were certainly not welcomed by the bottling works that had to insert corks to seal their vessels once filled. It has been estimated that an experienced glassblower working with four assistants might be able to produce about 200 good-quality bottles in a fourteen-hour day.

The other issue was the strength of the glass itself. Still beverages or uncarbonated patent medicines did not require a particularly strong bottle. In the 19th century Northeast, bottles for commercial products came from far and wide with manufacturers drawing from differing qualities of source materials, typically quartz-rich sands or rock formations. The relatively easily-made square or rectangular glass bottles used for most patent medicines, food flavorings, shoe polish, and other household products of the day were quite sufficient. However, for bottles intended to retain a pressurized liquid, the physics of material science dictates they need to be rounded.[44]

Soda fountain entrepreneur Gustavus Dows was reportedly the first to import bottled ginger ale to the United States in 1861. Typically, the early imports of carbonated mineral waters and then flavored sodas such as ginger ale from across the Atlantic Ocean arrived in America in thick-walled round-bottom bottles. Some products, especially ginger ales, were often contained in "torpedo" shaped glass bottles. Storing the merchandise on their sides helped prevent the corks from drying out and losing all the product's fizz.

Bottlers in this country adopted these strange ovoid bottles that were considered awkward to store and use but represented the best that early and mid-1800s technology had to offer.

Finding suitable closures for bottles with pressurized liquids was another matter. The age-old standby was of course natural cork shaped into a plug. Good quality corks were relatively inexpensive, especially for use on a low-cost item like water or soda.[45] Also, as with bottling Champagne, carbonated spring and mineral waters as well as the flavored sodas required a string or wire attachment to hold the cork in place, sometimes with the additional aid of a wax seal. In a simple, low-volume bottling situation the operator would place a pre-soaked cork on each filled bottle and force the cork in place with some well-positioned whacks from a wooden mallet, then affix a wire closure on top. Production rates were severely limited by these methods.

> By 1892, more than 1,500 patents were registered in the United States alone for various types of soda bottle closures.
> Source: Witzel and Young-Witzel, 1998.

In a more mechanized set-up for a flavored soda product, an operator of an early style bottling machine dispensed syrup and carbonated water directly into each new bottle on a line by controlling a foot pedal. The syrup gauge could be set to dispense the exact amount of syrup called for in the beverage recipe. The operator inserted a soaked cork into the machine's cylinder and then his instructions might read:

> Release the foot pedal sufficiently allowing the bottling cylinder to rise, meanwhile holding down the cork with your hand, put the wire bail securely over the cork.
>
> Remove your foot from the pedal and you can remove your filled bottle from the filling machine.[46]

Like the glassblower, the bottling operator had to possess training as well as skill to be successful. Production rates for such operations still left a lot to be desired.

By the 1870s bottlers had several other closure choices other than cork: the Codd ball stopper, with an internal marble holding back the content's pressure, and the more versatile and popular Swing stoppers with either a metal or porcelain cap and gasket, or the Hutchinson style internal stopper on a bail. Each had some advantages and disadvantages. The Swing stopper (also called a Lightning stopper) facilitated reuse, as cleaning was fairly straight-forward and many breweries of the era preferred this type of bottle and closure.

Bottles were another matter that the carbonated beverage industry struggled with throughout the 19th century. Hand-blown bottles varied in wall thickness and therefore could be unpredictable regarding the pressures they could withstand. In the summer months, when filled bottles of carbonated beverages are exposed to direct sunlight or warehouse heat, the internal pressures could easily reach 100 pounds.[47] This is not a problem for modern glass soda bottles but was definitely a hazard with the hand-blown bottles of the earlier era.

To make matters worse, new glass bottles straight from the factory had a tendency to be brittle. This led to excess breakage during the washing, filling, capping, labeling and packaging stages, or simply led to the bottles' inability to contain the carbonation pressures required of them. Aged bottles could greatly improve in strength, but maintaining a large inventory of glass just sitting in storage "aging" was not an appealing option to any manufacturer striving to be profitable.[48]

The decade of the 1890s in America is considered a golden age for many diverse reasons. Commonly referred to as The Gay Nineties or The Gilded

Age, it was period of changes in fashion, culture, and economics that were complemented by the creative proliferation of inventions and advancements in automobiles, air craft and medicine. The 1890s were truly a watershed decade for the soft drink bottling industry as well, with technological advancements and improved handling processes that carry on up to today's modern beverage operations.

A prolific Baltimore inventor, Irish-born American William Painter had a better idea for a bottle closure. In 1892 he patented a "crown cork" that he first created three years earlier and the Crown Cork & Seal Company (now called Crown Holdings) was off and running. However, Painter's small metal crimped cap with its thin cork inner liner was not an instant success in the marketplace for a couple of reasons.

Initially there was skepticism in the soft drink and beer bottling sector that a thin piece of metal and cork could serve the intended purpose of retaining high pressures. In the 1890s existing bottlers had invested in inventories of certain bottle types, most commonly those using Hutchinson or Swing/Lightning stoppers. All of their production equipment was specific to the cleaning, filling, capping and labeling these bottle types. Scrapping perfectly good equipment and replacing them with crown cork-compatible machinery was a costly endeavor for any type of business, especially for the small neighborhood bottlers. Second, just as Painter's "better mouse trap" entered the market, the country was struck with the economic panic of 1893 and muddled through a three-year recession, considerably slowing the industry's adoption of the crown bottle cap.

Unrelated to the development of the crown cork, but also totally aligned with similar American ingenuity, Toledo (Ohio) Glass Company employee Michael Owens was tackling the bottle problem. His company responsibilities taught him first-hand the difficulties of making quality beverage bottles with manufactured consistency. In 1895 he patented a semi-automatic machine for making blow-molded glass bottles, and by 1903 he founded the Owens Bottle Machine Company. His fully automated bottle machine worked on a circular rotating framework and could produce four bottles per second at an 80 percent labor savings.

A marriage was now made in heaven. Owen's equipment turned out inexpensive, consistently- strong beverage bottles in great quantities while Painter's crown corks provided an equally advantageous and universal closure. The combination of technologies took the industry by storm and as bottling works adapted, the commercial potential of the spring water and soft drink industries became enormous.

> With the demise of the cork stopper and other closure devices and the growing popularity of the metal bottle crowns after about 1910, bottlers now had a surface on which they could designate their product's flavor to the consuming public.
> Source: Riley, 1972

The United States had a total of 123 bottling plants in 1860 at the start of the Civil War. By 1870 there were 387 bottling plants, by 1880 that had climbed to 512, and by 1890 the country counted 1,377 individual plants with an estimated annual production of over $14 million. The number of plants doubled by the end of the century to 2,763 with over $23 million in production revenues. The start of the 20th century was primed for the explosive growth of bottled waters and sodas of all types. Some would find success, and their brands are well known to us today. Many more, though, had a local or regional customer base and succumbed to the difficulties inherent to any consumer-oriented business: market recognition, production efficiency, distribution logistics, worthy competition, and other factors.

* * *

LEARNING CURVES AND INNOVATORS

When all is said and done, it's all about the customer. Both soda fountain operators and bottlers of carbonated drinks, like any good merchants even in the 19th century, keenly understood this truism: If the customer isn't satisfied, if your product is only "average" or deemed not a particularly good value for the money, or if you have quality issues, you likely don't have a business with any serious longevity.

One factor of quality and economics that flavored soda producers came to understand was there is no value in over-carbonating the product during the bottling operation. Excess CO_2 quickly escapes after bottles are opened and the liquid content rapidly equilibrates. As early as 1882, carbonated beverage advisor Thomas Chester coached that for most sodas the optimal finished bottling pressure was in the range of 30 to 50 pounds (per square inch). This range is not far off from typical guidance used by soda bottling industry some sixty years later–a recommended 20 to 40 pounds. Different types of beverages or different flavors often have different optimal pressures, thus accounting for the range rather than a single fixed target.

As competition for the public's business grew, the list of possible flavors for carbonated soft drinks, either dispensed at the soda fountain or in a bottle became nearly endless. In his *History of the American Soft Drink Industry*, John Riley lists at least seventy varieties—not company brands but actual different flavors or branded specialty flavors ("Goldenade" anyone? It's a combination of lemon and egg flavorings.) Most every soda fountain proprietor or soft drink bottler also had their own flavored concoctions popular with their local clientele (and more profitable to them than purchasing branded syrups from the likes of Coca-Cola or Moxie). Lemon soda, sarsaparilla, root beer and ginger ale were the most popular flavors in the last third of the 19th century. In 1871 the owners of Lemon's Superior Sparkling Ginger Ale were granted this country's first trademark registration for a soft drink.

Figure 6 Vintage sign in a New Hampshire antique shop advertising a Luncheonette establishment. Note in the Tonics choices that only Coca-Cola and Moxie brands are specifically named.

Delightfully, the public had a downright dizzying choice for fizzy soft drinks. As equipment costs dropped and the bottle and closure problems were solved, the country saw an explosion of mom & pop operations. Without very much capital investment, an enterprising individual could set up a hometown bottling operation in their garage, shed, or leased warehouse space. Their typical customers were the small neighborhood grocers, the local eateries, and often the walk-ins from the surrounding residential blocks. Of the perhaps 30,000 bottlers that plied their trade in the United States, the vast majority are relegated to history. In the 'where are they now' category, how many have heard of:

- Grapine
- Orange Whistle
- Celery Cola
- Kola Ade
- Bluebird
- Smile-O

- TruAde
- O-So Grape
- Tangerette
- Wiseola
- Circle A Ginger Ale
- Zing Zoda

Or any of the over one thousand other soda brands that have come and gone from the scene?

Why did some brands thrive and others fade out of existence? Who were the early innovators that are still around today? We'll take a brief look at four survivors who started in business prior to 1890: Hires, Moxie, Dr Pepper and Coca-Cola.

HIRES ROOT BEER

Root Beer is, of course, made with roots! Just like the myriad of home-concocted medicinals, root beer as a drink has its early origins in colonial America, typically as "root tea" and served hot. But it took a Philadelphia pharmacist, Charles E. Hires, to develop a winning recipe and capitalize on it with strong commercial sales. In 1870 Hires was in an experimental frame of mind and through trial and error settled on a combination of roots, herbs and berries as the "just right" blend for the human palate. His recipe included sassafras, wintergreen, juniper berries, vanilla bean, licorice and eleven other ingredients.[49] The pharmacist called his choice mixture Hires' Root Tea (or Herb Tea) and began to sell it from his apothecary shop.

Somewhere on his road to fame and fortune, Hires was convinced to exchange the "tea" for "beer" in his beverage's name, and he also began to prepare and package his dry ingredients for home brewing. The home brewer only had to add sugar, water, yeast (to create the fizz) and time to produce their own consistently high-quality refreshment. With his tasty formula and packaged approach, Hires distributed samples at the 1876 Philadelphia Centennial Exposition and soon after began selling the dried preparation via mail followed by a liquid extract version in 1880.

Hires' marketing sense led him to advertise his product in such popular venues at the *Ladies' Home Journal* and *Harper's Weekly*. His ads quite naturally touted his "delicious, sparkling and wholesome" beverage. Reflecting his pharmacist training and his 19th century world view, the ads also reminded the would-be buyers of the drink's herbal impact: "Soothing to the nerves, vitalizing to the blood, refreshing to the brain, beneficial in every way." Hires purposely pitched his drink to the followers of the national Temperance Movement as a perfect non-alcoholic choice for the home. Many women enthusiastically heard his message and responded by purchasing his product[50].

Figure 7 Not commercially carbonated and bottled until 1893, Hire's Root Beer extract was immediately popular with soda fountain proprietors and home brewers following its introduction in the 1870s.

Hires' Improved Root Beer was wildly popular by 1890, but it still wasn't available at the local soda fountain, let alone by bottle, until 1893. Loyal followers could now pick up the favorite beverage ready-to-drink at their neighborhood grocer. Expanding sales beyond the Philadelphia market, Hires Root Beer would go on to become the nation's favorite root beer soda.[51]

MOXIE

While American druggists and pharmacists were turning their laboratory skills into creating new beverages for the soda fountain or home brew market, a genuine physician believed he had a better way. Dr. Augustin Thompson was born in Union, Maine and served with decorated honors in the Civil War. Graduating from Philadelphia's Hahnemann Homeopathia College in 1867, Thompson established a thriving medical practice in the bustling manufacturing community of Lowell, Massachusetts. He may well have been drawn to the Mill City in part because it was a known center for remedies and patent medicines. Lowell was home to the wildly successful J.C. Ayer & Company as well as the C.I Hood & Company, both with extensive lines of nationally-known products pitched as useful health aides and cures.

As a well-established physician and proponent of homeopathic medicines, Thompson may well have concocted various syrups or cordials and provided them to his patients to treat their ailments. Many physicians did just that. What is known for certain is that in March 1885 Moxie Nerve Food was made available to the general public by the bottle. A frequently claim is that Thompson first created his extract in 1876, a "fact" repeated by dozens of authors and publications since the early 1980s. This date could possibly be true, but there is zero factual evidence to support it.[52]

As a physician, Thompson purposed to develop a beverage that was devoid of the harmful substances contained in many remedies of his day, including the ever-popular bitters which could contain in excess of 40 percent alcohol. The patent application of the same year stated, "Has not a drop of Medicine, Poison, Stimulant, or Alcohol in its composition." All true actually.

The ingredients in Moxie Nerve Food were, in fact, quite similar to those found in a number of root beers of the day, but with one added secret ingredient. This mysterious ingredient was initially part of the "mystique" that Thompson quite purposely created at the launching of his proprietary beverage. His product launch incorporated the wild tale of a former Army comrade, one "Lt. Moxie," who brought Thompson his discovery of a strange South American plant with wonderful, health-infused properties. Secret ingredients have always been beneficial to boosting product sales, but the constituent which gave Moxie Nerve Food its unique and somewhat bitter or medicine-like flavor was the rather well-known gentian root.[53]

Gentian leaves and roots are harvested in several locales; the most commercially available, even in Thompson's day, are imported from parts of France and Spain. Gentian extract remains in Moxie soda's formulation up to the present time. However, many non-Moxie drinkers will have consumed the herb as a key ingredient in the popular Angostura Bitters, available in virtually any U.S. grocery store. In herbal medicine applications, gentian is commonly recommended as a remedy for digestion problems, fever, hypertension and loss of appetite.

Thompson discovered early on the bitter flavor imparted by gentian could be minimized if the finished beverage was served ice cold and highly charged with CO_2, at a much higher pressure than most carbonated beverages of that time. Thompson mistrusted the neighborhood soda fountain proprietors to take proper care in preparing his drink at their counter services. He did sell syrup directly to these establishments but strongly preferred to sell Moxie Nerve Food bottled and then have attendants dispense glassfuls directly from ice-cold bottles. As a consequence, unlike his competitors, Thompson focused on producing and selling Moxie as a bottled beverage from the very start.

The desired high CO_2 pressures of Moxie Nerve Food presented a distinct challenge for 1885 technology. Hand-blown bottles of that era were often weak or just strong enough to contain lightly carbonated beverages with acceptable levels of breakage. Thompson solved his problem by contracting with the Lyndeborough Glass Company in southern New Hampshire. Lyndeborough was already supplying high quality glass bottles for Lowell's Hood's Sarsaparilla and the Lydia E. Pinkham Vegetable Compound, among others. The New Hampshire glassworks "secret" material was a local deposit of quartzite, a dense metamorphic rock derived from pure sandstone, recrystallized to interlock its grains and form incredible strength. Problem solved. The pure quartzite source rock also imparted an attractive blueish tint to the finished glass bottles (that would be much admired by serious bottle collectors a century later).

Figure 8 Examples of the distinctive aqua-blue glass produced by the Lyndeborough Glass Works in the late 1800s.

In addition to being an accomplished physician, Augustin Thompson was also a published playwright and put his literary skills to good use in marking his new beverage. At first, the campaigns relied heavily on newspaper advertising, but before the end of the century Thompson would pioneer a wealth of attention-getting novelties. One such item was a giant wooden replica Moxie bottled pulled by a horse-drawn carriage from which a uniformed attendant could pour customers an ice-cold glass of carbonated refreshment.

Sales of Moxie Nerve Food skyrocketed in its home territory of New England, and by the close of its first year, 1885, the brand was virtually a house-hold name. The following year company literature stated that five million bottles had been sold within the first fourteen months of operation. This validity of this claim is quite doubtful, but it is a fact that Moxie's early success was unparalleled in the fledgling beverage industry, and sales continued their steep climb for the rest of the century and into the next. This bitter-sweet tasting concoction continues to have a loyal following today and remains the oldest continuously-bottled carbonated soft drink in America.

Illustration 7 Early advertisement for Moxie carbonated beverage.

DR PEPPER

In the late 1800s one of the largest pharmacies in central Texas was the Old Corner Drug Store in Waco. However, it wasn't the just medicinal wares that drew in the crowds, it was also the elaborate soda fountain that provided the main attraction. One of the establishment's ambitious employees was Charles C. Alderton, a medical school graduate who observed that customers at the soda fountain often requested different blends of syrups and flavorings. Experimenting in late 1885, Alderton came up with a unique mixture of twenty-three ingredients that appeared dark like a cola, but had a distinctive cherry-fruity taste.

Alderton's beverage creation proved extremely popular and was originally called "A Waco" by locals after their home town. But the store's owner, Wade Morrison, eventually started advertising this popular flavor as "Dr Pepper," reportedly named in honor of his former employer and the father of his long-lost love back in Virginia.

Alderton created his unique syrup blend in the same year that Moxie Nerve Food was commercialized but a full year before Pemberton created his Coca-Cola temperance drink. From the beginning, like Moxie, Dr Pepper was advertised as different from a cola and containing none of that (evil) caffeine or any unhealthy ingredients. But similar to Moxie Nerve Food and Coca-Cola, Dr Pepper's advertisements would claim various health benefits from imbibing, including curing nervousness, sleeplessness, stomach ailments, and hangovers, while delivering the drink's patron an all-around youthful feeling. "Vim, Vigor, Vitality, Satisfaction in Every Glass" read one print advertisement of the day.

Dr Pepper was initially only available as a fountain drink, either at the Old Corner Drug Store or at establishments that purchased the formular's syrup by the gallon. The bottling of this product did not commence until 1888 at the earliest (some sources date the start of commercial bottling at 1891). Eventually, owner Wade Morrison formed a partnership with another Texas beverage chemist who worked to perfect the original formula, and they began to produce the popular Dr Pepper in quantity and expand the product's geographical reach.[54]

COCA-COLA

As early as 1881, American soda fountains were offering various prepared beverages with ingredients derived from coca leaves and kola nuts (or seeds). Coca leaves contain alkaloids including traces of cocaine, and kola seeds harbor a distinctive bitter flavor and contain between 2 to 4% caffeine. Both of these plants, just like the coffee berry, already had a long history of use in various world cultures and in Western herbal applications.

In 1850 a Georgia native named John S. Pemberton earned a degree from the Reform Medical College of Georgia, which followed the therapeutic principles of Thomsonian Medicine (discussed in Chapter 2). There he specialized in chemistry and the study of botanicals. After obtaining a pharmacist license, he opened a drug store in his hometown of Columbus, Georgia, where he demonstrated his passion for developing remedies and elixirs of his own design. Once his service to the Confederacy during the American Civil War was satisfied, Pemberton moved to Atlanta where he created proprietary medical formulations and pursued his quest for a breakthrough product that would bring him fame and fortune.

Ironically, one of Pemberton's first successful products brought him far from the teachings instilled within the Thomsonian system of therapeutics. He developed a variation on a well-known European recipe of the time–a sugary wine and coca cordial widely sold as Vin Mariani. Pemberton's version, French Wine of Coca, was enthusiastically received by Atlanta consumers in 1885 as "an ideal nerve tonic and stimulant." Maybe it was indeed. But when the City of Atlanta and Fulton County enacted temperance legislation the very next year, Pemberton had to rethink and reformulate his most popular product.

By eliminating the wine and adding other flavorings, Pemberton formulated a non-alcoholic version of his French Wine of Coca and convinced his druggist friend at nearby Jacob's Pharmacy to try it at their fountain service. History is somewhat muddy as to whether it was Pemberton himself or his druggist friend who first mixed the new syrup with carbonated water. Either way, the drink introduced in 1886 was an unqualified hit among the fountain's customers, tasting distinctly different from the ginger ales, fruity drinks, and root beers they were accustomed to being served.

Most credit for the alliterative name Coca-Cola is given to one of Pemberton's business partners, Maine-born Frank Robinson. The now-famous Coca-Cola logotype with its flowing script is also attributed to Robinson. Not a bad contribution to the rolls of soft drink antiquity on the part of a Yankee accountant from East Corinth, Maine!

With Pemberton's failing health and eventual passing in the summer of 1888, the ownership and control of the fledgling business was acquired by another Atlanta druggist, Asa Candler. Candler partnered with Frank Robinson in 1892 to form a new company, the Coca-Cola Company, with a decidedly aggressive orientation toward both marketing and rapid geographical expansion. Typical of the era, and especially of rival Moxie, the advertising for Coke continued to reflect mixed messages of the drink as a refreshment as well as an aid to health and wellbeing.

Coca-Cola was strictly a fountain drink at this time, and Candler and Robinson focused heavily on syrup sales and distribution. It was a Vicksburg, Mississippi candy company that first bottled the Atlanta-born beverage in March 1894 (some nine years after the introduction of Moxie Nerve Food and several years following the introduction of bottled Dr Pepper). Convinced of the soft drink's appeal, the Biedenham Candy Company used Hutchison-type bottles to get its wares out to the rural sections of Vicksburg and beyond.

Illustration 8 Coca-Cola was not the only soft drink with an extensive advertising campaign, but they were acknowledged leaders. Image adapted from a 1980 Jerry Miller note card.

Understanding that the future of branded syrup sales was in franchising, Candler and Robinson sold bottling rights to two Chattanooga, Tennessee entrepreneurs for one dollar. Thus, that southern city won the right to establish the first Coca-Cola Bottling Company with the Atlanta enterprise content to make and sell the syrup. This style of franchise model would prove to be not only good for the Coca-Cola Company but also become a major headache as the national, and then international, demand for the product grew[55].

A NEW ERA DAWNS

The bottling of flavored carbonated soft drinks was still a relatively immature business sector at the start of the 20th century. Syrup and bottling plants were small and primarily producing their own brands and flavors oriented toward their local markets. The 1890s were the formative years when the concept of franchising and market expansion took a firm hold. The dominance of the big national brands was far in the future, but the seeds planted in the 1890s were beginning to blossom. National legislation against quack medicines, the growing temperance movement and changing public tastes would all play a large role in the development and maturing of the carbonated soda business.

4 EARLY FIZZ IN THE GRANITE STATE: 1880-1950

1906 FOOD AND DRUGS ACT BRINGS CHANGE

Chapter 2 discussed the fact that patent medicines were not legally patented at all but were proprietary formulations. Essentially, nothing controlled or regulated what could be offered for public consumption by non-physicians, and nothing prohibited wild claims concerning product effectiveness. Newspapers and magazines of 19th century North America derived substantial advertising revenues from the merchants who manufactured and offered such remedies and elixirs. In actuality, most of these publications were quite eager to avoid any discussion of potential harm to the general public posed by product ingredients advertised in their pages.

The winds of change started to stir in the 1890s. Edward William Bok was a successful publisher who focused heavily on women and women's issues. As editor of the *Ladies' Home Journal*, in 1892 Bok announced that the publication would cease accepting advertising from the patent medicine sector, helping to turn public sentiment toward thinking that reforms were needed.

President Calvin Coolidge was known to be fond of soft drinks and served them often in the White House. Vermonter Calvin Coolidge was Vice President when Warren G. Harding died in office. At his home in Plymouth Notch, Coolidge was sworn in as President in the middle of the night. He promptly honored the historic occasion by enjoying a Moxie soda before retiring for the balance of the night.

Substantial change in the patent medicine and food and beverage sectors was close at hand when a crusading pure-foods chemist, Harvey W. Wiley, was appointed to what would become the federal Food and Drug Administration. Wiley's tenacious efforts to protect the consuming public led to passage of watershed legislation known simply as the Food and Drugs Act (or "Wiley Act"), which was signed into law in 1906 by President Teddy Roosevelt. While the law did not ban harmful product ingredients outright, it did regulate advertising claims and served as a clear directive for the patent medicine, beverage, and food industries to initiate serious changes.

A number of highly-promoted beverage brands at the turn of the century, in fact, purposely bridged the dual worlds of patent medicine and healthy refreshment. Probably the most notable examples among the already successful brands with still-growing reputations was Coca-Cola and Moxie. Arguably, each had a great deal to lose if they lost the public's trust and favor. In 1907 Moxie dropped "Nerve Food" from its trademark filings, stating simply that it provided "a non-alcoholic carbonated beverage and syrup for making the same."

Coca-Cola also saw the changes coming in both public opinion and in the heavy-hand of federal regulation and removed saccharin (which provided a cost savings over cane sugar) from its flagship drink's formula. The product was then actively promoted as a Great National Temperance Beverage that "aids digestion and...gives a zest for additional labor and a keener enjoyment of recreation." Temperance advocates[56] were not fully won over, however, since Coca-Cola's formula still contained caffeine. Of course, it was well known that tea and coffee naturally contained caffeine, but these beverages were not widely marketed to both adults and the youth. Coke was.

* * *

ADVANCES AND CHALLENGES

Advances in bottles and closures and plant bottling equipment, and their adoption by even the small bottlers, helped to meet the growing consumer demand for carbonated soft drinks of all types. In addition to the brands already mentioned, Pepsi-Cola, Clicquot Club, Barq's Root Beer, Vernors Ginger Ale and others with staying power entered the marketplace alongside of the pervasive mom & pop-produced sodas. By 1910, the U.S. counted some 4,916 production plants cranking out mineral waters and fizzy bottled drinks. Ginger ale led the list

Dry Ginger Ale became popular in the 1920s and with National Prohibition and the Canada Dry brand was initially imported from Toronto in 1921. Dry Ginger Ale is lighter in sugar content and heavier in lemon flavoring than a Golden Ginger Ale.
Source: Riley, 1972.

of the most popular flavors in addition to the colas, sarsaparillas and root beers. But other consumer must-haves included ginger beer, birch beer, orange, cherry smash, cream (vanilla), lemon and strawberry.[57]

Soft drink production was still primarily a summertime venture, and in the Northeast many bottling plants would shutter their doors come Labor Day, waiting for next year's warmth to restart the public's thirst for ice-cold (non-alcoholic) refreshments. The increasing popularity of outdoor recreation, destination resorts, and the mobility afforded by the motor car certainly helped to increase the overall demand for summer soft drinks. Also, the replacement of the bottler's horse-drawn delivery wagon with petroleum-fired trucks like the Mack, White, International Harvester, and others greatly facilitated product distribution.

With the entry of the United States into World War I in 1917, soft drink ingredients became harder to procure as well as more expensive. The end of the Great War and installation of Prohibition provided a tremendous boost for the sale all types of non-alcoholic beverages. The always-popular soda fountain came into its glory years during Prohibition. Their counter seating and booths replaced the bar stool as the preferred social meeting place. The skilled bartender was now the skilled soda jerk. By the end of the 1920s the United States could boast of its 120,000 soda fountains coast to coast. New York City alone had some 650 establishments.

The 1920s and 1930s were also the decade when soft drink promotion and advertising came into its own, especially with the use of radio. Clicquot Club (started in Millis, Massachusetts) was one of the first brands to employ radio advertising by broadcasting its "Eskimo" overture of 1925 to its thirsty listeners. Pepsi-Cola was perhaps the first soft drink company to advertise using a sky-writing airplane in 1938. The growing American beverage industry was prominently displayed during the World's Fair held in Chicago during 1933-34 where attendees could marvel at a fully-equipped bottling plant that produced an astounding 120 bottles of carbonated refreshment every minute.

Through the early 1950s, the universal container for carbonated sodas was of course the humble glass bottle, designed primarily for single-serving individual consumption. Many bottlers attempted to create container shapes for their flagship products that would distinguish the brand in the minds and wallets of the consumer. This was typically true of most patent medicines and many of the early bottled beverages of all types. Before and after the turn of the century, Moxie successfully won several court battles against would-be copy-cats, in part by arguing their high-shoulder bottle design was unique and fully identifiable with the brand in the public's eyes.

Like many patent medicine manufacturers, beer makers, and others, bottlers of spring waters and flavored sodas commonly contracted with their glass works to emboss their company name on their wares. The glass makers carved the information onto a metal "slug plate" which was then inserted into a generic bottle mold, usually one made of carved wood. When the molten glass was poured into the mold during the forming process, the slug plate would emboss its identifying information onto the bottle. Information might also include the bottler's city or the container's fluid capacity, but not typically specific flavors. The finished product's flavor was most often identified either by paper labels on the bottles, or later through information contained on the painted cork-lined crown cap. Such caps have long been prized by modern soft drink memorabilia collectors, especially if the surviving caps are uncrimped (never applied to bottles during the course of a production run).

In spite of its's readily-identifiable script logo, Coca-Cola continued to be concerned with fighting off imitators, and in 1915 its lead attorney encouraged the company to develop a unique bottle design as well. Some eight to ten U.S. glass manufacturers were asked to submit designs for consideration, and in early 1916 Coke selected the Root Glass Company of Indiana and their unique "hobbleskirt" design.[58] Coca-Cola's new bottle achieved the company's objective and became instantly recognizable by consumers. By 1920 most bottled Coca-Cola product used this distinctive bottle and a variation of that shape remains in use today. The 1920-1930 decade saw literally hundreds of bottlers borrowing from Coke's idea and producing their own version of unique and proprietary shapes and surface textures: Whistle, Orange Crush, Kist, Dr Pepper, and Howdy among them.

> Coca-Cola in bottles was first featured in newspaper advertising in 1902. The company's advertising budget for that year was about $100,000.
> Source: Riley, 1972.

The glass industry pioneered a major technological advancement in the 1930s by creating a colored label using borosilicate and mineral pigments permanently fused onto the bottle. Starting commercially in 1934, Applied Color Labels, or ACLs, provided soda bottlers (and to a lesser extent milk bottlers) with an attractive option for capturing market share with bright eye-appealing "painted" labels. The ACL also had the advantage of unmistakable, permanent identity thereby preventing competitors from "misappropriating" a company's bottles for their own re-use. As a result of this advancement, many bottlers quickly moved away from their elaborately shaped or textured bottles which required the use of more costly specialty molds. ACL bottles from the 1930s, 40s and 50s are eagerly sought by collectors for their attractiveness and the story they can tell through product names and bottling locations.

Clicquot Club captured another first in the flavored soda industry. It was the very first brand to sell ginger ale in cone-top cans (although Coca-Cola also experimented with these cone-tops in the 1930s). The 1936 trial was abandoned by Clicquot Club after just one year, partly because of seam-sealing problems due to the carbonated contents. Additionally, the available technology for coating the can's inner surfaces to prevent interactions with most food and beverages was not sufficiently advanced. Interactions of the product with the can's metal affected taste, especially when highly-acidic fruits, vegetables, and beverages were involved. World War II and its accompanying metal shortages put a hold to any further technological developments and soda bottlers continued to employ their reliable standby—the glass bottle.

As the U.S. public became more mobile and travel to the suburbs and the countryside became popular, roadside stores and filling stations sported conveniently-placed soda coolers filled with cracked ice and soft drinks in bottles. Most were simply open-top tubs with ice replenished by the store's attendants from bulk deliveries supplied by the local ice man. Typically, these point-of-purchase dispensers worked on the honor system as the patrons grabbed "a cold one" and paid their nickel to the store's proprietor. These commercial "appliances" also served as highly-visible brand advertising space, something that Coca-Cola was especially adept at using to maintain visibility with the public and hopefully gain market share.

Figure 9 Lucille's Variety on Brook St. in Manchester was a typical neighborhood store where the Coca-Cola cooler was on prominent display. Customers and newly-weds Joseph and Rita Bennett pose ca. 1946. Note the Moxie sign in the upper left rafters. Credit: Susan Bennett Byrd.

The first fully-commercial, self-contained, coin-operated bottled soda drink dispenser was created in 1936-37 by the newly-formed Vendo Company of Kansas City. Elmer F. Pierson and three associates set out to make and market a vending top for existing Coca-Cola coolers in use at that time. The unit was made by the Mills Novelty Company and sold and placed in some 3,000 locations within the first year. By the time production was halted by the redirection of American manufacturing to war goods for World War II, tens of thousands of these units were familiar sights across the country.[59] The introduction of upright stand-alone bottle-dispensing units occurred with the onset of the post-war economic boom and the company's successor is still operating today (as SandenVendo America, Inc. in Dallas, TX).

Coming out of the Great Recession and then World War II, the country's collective thirst for soft drinks was clearly growing. In October 1940 the *Portsmouth Herald* reported that New England alone boasted over 800 bottling plants for carbonated beverages, most of which were still locally-owned and operated. World War II of course brought a wide variety of material shortages to the beverage industry as it did with other consumer goods in the United States. There were shortages of cork for the crown cap liners, paperboard for cartons, tires for delivery trucks, metal for bottle caps, coolers and vending machines and, most limiting, the severe rationing of sugar. The overall restrictive effects on the industry were substantial at a time when soft drinks were desired in great quantities by war production plants, military training centers, and for shipment overseas to the fighting troops.

> In 1940 the per capita annual consumption of carbonated sodas in the U.S. reached the 100-drink mark.
> Source: Riley, 1972.

This challenge led to significant creativity on the part of the syrup producers and bottlers. The "Moxieland" central plant in Boston attempted to use blackstrap molasses as a substitute for cane sugar, even though their own chemist warned management that the sweetener was already fermenting in the storage barrels. Management ignored the warning and put up a hundred thousand cases of Moxie using the molasses–with disastrous results. Bottles exploded and even indiscriminating kids found the beverage to be undrinkable. Everything that was bottled had to be destroyed and written off as a total loss.

Glass plants, like most material-intensive manufactures, were working twenty-four hours a day during the war years to produce glass containers. Great quantities were needed not simply for the normal consumer demands, but food and beverage producers needed to shift away from utilizing metal cans since that material was prioritized for the military.

New Hampshire's soft drink bottlers, not surprisingly, had difficulties in getting their empties returned from their overseas shipments to military bases. This situation simply added to the dire shortage of available reusable glass bottles. An article in the August 12, 1943, *Portsmouth Herald* headlined: "Scour Your Attics for Bottles, Jars." The article went on to explain:

> Soft drink bottlers urge, beg and plead with you to get those "slacker" bottles out of hiding. They ask you to do this for your own good as well as for your neighbors, service men and all lovers of soft drinks....The refunded bottle deposits may amount to almost what you need to finish your War Savings Stamp Book.

Participation in metal and glass salvage drives, War Bond campaigns, and other home front programs became part of the soda bottlers' contributions to the war effort. With the war's end and the lifting of most restrictions (sugar was still rationed for some time), a thousand new bottling plants were added in the U.S. between 1946 and 1949 alone. The franchised brands were growing the fastest, often to the detriment of the small regional or local bottler.

* * *

EARLY NEW HAMPSHIRE BOTTLERS

The ending to the U.S. Civil War and a return to peacetime saw numerous spring water and carbonated soda bottlers open for business in New Hampshire. With few exceptions, these early bottling works were primarily small operations serving up home-made formulations to their local communities. Undoubtedly many of these small bottlers had a loyal following, but most did not survive in business for more than a few years. Perhaps many offered inferior products, were unreliable suppliers to their merchants, or were beset by some ill fortunes. A respected reference source on this industry[60] indicates that at least fifty-four New Hampshire firms were started between the Civil War period and 1900 with the purpose of bottling water or flavored soda. Yet the U.S. Census from 1900 reported only seven bottling plants operating in the State of New Hampshire and they employed a mere thirty-two workers in total.

Figure 10 Manchester Tonic Co. represented the myriad of smaller bottlers that thrived at one time. Operating from 1924 until 1938, it sold its own line of soft drinks as well as Squeeze, a brand from the Massachusetts Berkshire region. Credit: Manchester Historic Association.

Illustration 9 Paper label for Kleer-Kool Beverages, a product of the Manchester Tonic Co.

An additional sixty-four New Hampshire bottlers opened for business between 1900 and 1920, demonstrating a growing consumer sector and a faith in their particular products. National Prohibition came through the Eighteenth Amendment in 1919 and was a powerful boost to non-alcoholic beverage sales of all types. This was especially true for bottled carbonated sodas, whose sales rose some 200 percent throughout the Prohibition years. However, the onset of the Great Depression sweeping the country, coupled with the repeal of National Prohibition in 1933, brought great uncertainty to the soft beverage industry. Many of the plants that had brewed and bottled beer prior to Prohibition often switched back to making this profitable alcoholic brew. In some case the plants maintained their soda line, but more commonly the soft drinks were sidelined and the precious production capacity used to maximize the output of beer. Even the growing soft drink powerhouse Coca-Cola briefly toyed with the idea of developing a post-Prohibition line of bottled beers.

Many of the smaller New Hampshire soda bottlers simply did not survive once National Prohibition was lifted. Of course, some merged with other bottlers or became contract bottlers for one of the national brands (often times still bottling their own local brands or flavors). Many more just simply ceased production and closed their doors. From the 1860s up through today at least 205 separate bottlers in sixty cities and towns have tried to make their mark in the Granite State. Manchester has seen at least forty-three of these enterprises, Nashua twenty, Portsmouth and Dover twelve each and even the Laconia area birthed at least eight bottlers during this period.[61]

> In 1922 New Hampshire boasted 41 bottlers of soda, tonics or spring water.

The following table provides a sampling of just some of the early bottlers of waters and flavored sodas in the Granite State.

Early NH Bottlers*

Company**	Location	Product(s)	Year Started	Year Closed
Granite State Spring Water Co.	Atkinson Depot/Plaistow	Spring water and sodas	1896	1928
City Bottling Co.	Berlin	Unknown	1905	1924
Aetna Bottling Co.	Concord	Flavored sodas	Pre 1885	1924
Granite Bottling Co.	Concord	Flavored sodas	Pre 1885	1929
Rumford Bottling Works	Concord	Flavored sodas	1904	1948
Whistle Bottling Co.	Concord	Flavored sodas & Coca-Cola	1920	1950
White Mountain Mineral Springs Water Co.	Conway	Spring water, mineral water, flavored sodas	1882	1929
Lafayette Bottling Co.	Derry (then Manch.)	Spring water and sodas	1906	1927
Daniel Ford, Bottler	Dover	Mineral water, sodas and beer	1866	1874
Henniker Spring Water Co.	Henniker	Spring water and mineral water	1874	1923
N.G. Gurnsey & Sons	Keene	Flavored sodas then Coca-Cola	Pre 1885	1972
Otto Lettenmayer, Bottler	Keene	Unknown	Pre 1885	1924
J.R. Champlin Soda Water Manufacturer	Laconia	Flavored sodas	1874	1906
Albany Steam Bottling Works	Manchester	Flavored sodas	1903	1906
D. Daoust	Manchester	Flavored sodas	1906	1926
Green Mountain Ginger Ale Co.	Manchester	Flavored sodas	1927	1949

Early Fizz in the Granite State: 1880-1950

Company**	Location	Product(s)	Year Started	Year Closed
Lafayette Bottling Co.	Manchester	Flavored sodas then Pepsi-Cola	Pre 1920	1972
Manchester Bottling Works/ W. F. Glancy	Manchester	Flavored sodas	1885	1920
Manchester Tonic Co/Marne River Tonic	Manchester	Flavored sodas	1919	1950
Joseph Quirin, Bottler	Manchester	Flavored sodas	1918	1922
Rock Spring & Bo La Co.	Manchester	Flavored sodas	1906	1965
Gustave Schneider Bottling Works	Manchester	Flavored sodas	Pre 1885	1950
J.A. Bellavance, Bottler	Nashua	Flavored sodas	Pre 1885	1916
J.J. McGlynn Bottling Works	Nashua	Flavored sodas	1916	1950
Simoneau Bottling Co.	Nashua	Flavored sodas	1922	1977
Conner Bottling Works	Newfields	Flavored sodas	1863	Operating
Newport Bottling Works	Newport	Flavored sodas	1916	1972
Boynton Bottling Works	Portsmouth	Flavored sodas then Coca-Cola	1873	1950
Laughlin Bottling Works	Portsmouth	Flavored sodas then Pepsi-Cola	1887	1972
Cocheco Bottling Works	Rochester	Flavored sodas	Pre 1900	1984
W.A. Horne Bottling Works	Somersworth	Flavored sodas then Canada Dry	1901	1949

* Far from an exhaustive list. The best source for a full compendium is Fewless and Weide, 2nd Ed., see Selected Bibliography. Exact dates of origin are often uncertain and dependent on the accuracy of available documentation such as published city directories, state business records or trade associations.

** Many companies used variations of their names or were purchased or merged. In general, the original names are listed here.

Relatively little is known for many of these New Hampshire enterprises, including their operations, sale volumes, and exact reasons for their demise. Many of them we know of only from listings in published city business directories, brief newspaper notations or advertisements, and (most frequently) from the resilient thick-walled returnable bottles that survive and are prized by soft drink collectors. Four of these former bottling enterprises are profiled below:

* * *

THE WHISTLE BOTTLING COMPANY, CONCORD

Whistle was a brand of orange soda developed by the Vess Company of St. Louis in 1916 and trademarked by the Orange Whistle Co. Other Whistle flavors were developed as well and Vess used contract bottlers or franchisees extensively. Reportedly, Whistle was bottled in 477 locations nationally, including in the Granite State by Robinson Bros. in Dover, Boynton Bottling Works in Portsmouth, Conner Bottling Works in Newfields, and the Whistle Bottling Co. of Concord.[62] City directories list the Concord operation as based at 125 N. Main St., the busy corner of Main and Loudon Rd./Centre St., but there are no known photographs of the original structure.

Exhibiting a diversity of brands and products that was characteristic of many small to medium size New Hampshire bottlers, the Concord operation also produced a Star Brand Ginger Ale and Imitation Strawberry (1920), a line of flavors called Granite State Beverages (1945-49), and served as a Coca-Cola bottler from about 1920 to 1937.

There is some dispute as to whether the Whistle Orange drink was created by company owner Vess Jones or his super-salesman, Charles Leiper Grigg. But it is known that Griggs left Vess' employment in 1919 and started his own beverage firm with a lightly carbonated orange soda he named Howdy. Grigg's version found reasonable success (and in NH was bottled by the Stark Spring Water Co. in W. Milan and the Queen City Bottling Works in Manchester), but it competed again a wealth of other orange beverages of the era, including the very popular Orange Crush.

Not one to give up his dream of soft drink success, Grigg's combined another highly popular flavor for sodas, lemon-lime, with a high level of carbonation. In a throw-back to the days of patent medicines, Grigg also added a small amount of lithium citrate to the blend. Lithium's use in pharmacology as an antidepressant only developed in the late 1940s, but Grigg launched his "Bib-labeled Lithiated Lemon-Line Soda" for public consumption in 1929. Grigg soon came to his better marketing senses and he renamed his drink 7Up. When Prohibition ended, he started promoting 7Up as a perfect mixer for use with any and all hard liquors. The added lithium was removed from the formulation in 1948 as that compound's validity as a *bona fide* medical aide became better understood by the profession.[63]

The Whistle Bottling Company of Concord closed operations in 1950 and the Whistle line of flavored sodas came under the national control of the Cott Corporation in 1994. The New Hampshire portion of the Cott story is profiled in Chapter 5.

* * *

N.G. GURNSEY & CO. BOTTLING WORKS, KEENE

The Gurnsey family were well-established business owners in the city of Keene by the second half of the 19th century. Norris G. Gurnsey of Winchester, New Hampshire, relocated to Keene in 1852 and started several restaurants in his newly-adopted community. By 1884 the Gurnsey family purchased an established bakery on the north corner of Main and Church Streets. They quickly became known as makers of the celebrated Keene (common) cracker, as well as other staples such as ginger snaps, soda crackers, tea biscuits, and graham crackers.[64]

N.G. Gurnsey & Co. was also bottling soft drinks by the early 1880s to complement their continuing restaurant business. Gurnsey-branded Hutchinson-style bottles are known to collectors, but only the beverage flavors from the crown cap era (post 1900) are known through surviving bottle caps. Collectors have documented Gurnsey Ginger Ale, Grape Whiz, Cream, Sarsaparilla and Imitation Orangeade through known bottle caps as well as an Orangeade paper label on a 7-oz clear glass bottle.

Records also show that N.G. Gurnsey later operated as a bottler for Hires Root Beer, Nu Grape products (1933-38) and eventually Coca-Cola products (1925-72). However, soft drink bottling under the Gurnsey family name appears to have ceased in 1961 with the sale of the Coca-Cola franchise to others who continued the operations as the Coca-Cola Bottling Co. of Keene. For a time in the 1940s, the N.G. Gurnsey Co., Inc. wholesaled tobacco, candy, and soda in Manchester at 293 Elm Street. Keene's Dunbar Street distribution operation (including Canada Dry products) continued until the company's dissolution in 2000.

Figure 11 N. G. Gurnsey & Co. Bottling Works operated at 88 Dunbar St. in Keene and produced beverages there from the mid 1920s until the early 1960s.

* * *

J.R. CHAMPLIN, LACONIA

With a business start date of 1874 (one source claims 1872), John (J.R.) Champlin of Laconia operated one of the earliest documented bottling works in the state of New Hampshire. Unfortunately, relatively little is known about this early Laconia enterprise – a not uncommon situation regarding the myriad of small bottling concerns. Business records do indicate that Champlin operated at 2 Water Street and later at 16 and 36 Court Street in the city. The 1880 census lists his profession as "Keeps saloon," while the 1900 census refers to him as a "bottler."

These census notations appear accurate as an 1877 newspaper advertisement from Champlin showcases a multitude of products and services including: mineral waters, aerated waters, Belfast Ginger Ale, Aerated Lemonade, Ottawa Beer, Coffee, and Spruce Beer. The same advertisement also proclaims, "Dealer in Lager Beer, Porter, Ale, Cider, Tobacco, Cigars, &c." Print ads from 1882 also list the availability of "Other Summer Beverages" which is indicative of the seasonality of the consumption of popular soft drinks and beers in New England.

Of special note is that by 1882 Champlin operated a wholesale and retail business serving a large portion of central and northern New Hampshire. His clientele included the regional soda fountain owners whom he provided with "charge," that is, bottled CO_2 to operate their establishments' carbonation equipment. In catering to the soda fountain trade, Champlin carried a line of "pure syrups at reasonable prices" and "Cheap Syrups made to order." Bottled flavored sodas of this period included Tonic, Lemon, Ginger Beer, Aerated Lemon, Sarsaparilla, Strawberry, Raspberry, and Pine Apple (not pineapple apparently!).

Surviving Champlin bottles of the Hutchinson type[65] are known to collectors and blob-top style clear bottles with Champlin's molded nameplate have been retrieved by SCUBA divers from the waters of Lake Winnipesaukee.

John Champlin appears to have been a diverse entrepreneur as he also directed the manufacture of iron hitching posts and telescopes at the Court Street location. An avid amateur astronomer, he reportedly also constructed an observatory on Jewett Hill in the city. Champlin passed in 1906, and the bottling business appears to have ceased operations in that same year.

* * *

GRANITE STATE SPRING WATER CO./OLD HAMPSHIRE, INC., ATKINSON DEPOT/PLAISTOW

M. Kimball Wentworth established the Granite State Spring Water Company in 1896 at 11 Wentworth Avenue in the western section of Plaistow, just north of the border with Haverhill, Massachusetts. Initially, the plant may have solely bottled spring waters since a 1911 report in *American Mineral Waters* indicates the spring was sampled in 1907 and found to have a flow of 500 gallons per hour at a water temperature of 40° F. The water was also found to be moderately mineralized with little or no bacteria, indicating "organic purity." There was no mention of this water source also being used to create flavored beverages.[66]

Mr. Wentworth drew heavily upon the image of Native Americans having visited this spring through the ages. Such imagery was frequently employed in those times by numerous bottling operations in New England and elsewhere. Surviving paper labels and embossing on glass bottles depicts two Native American men partaking of the spring with the caption: "And the Indians came here for pure water."

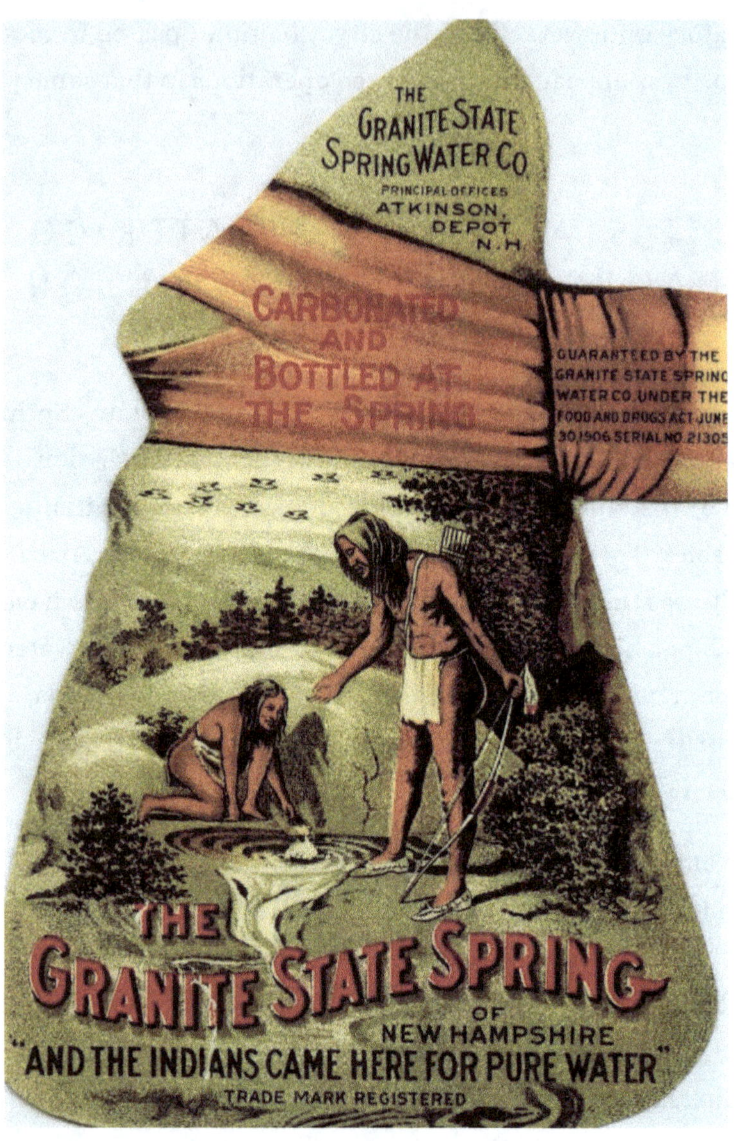

Illustration 10 The Granite State Spring Water Co. of Atkinson Depot also bottled Hi-Brown and Mar-Vo flavored sodas, often employing this same Native American image. The reference to the 1906 Food and Drug Act was a signal to the consumer that the company understood and followed the federal law.

Granite State Spring Water Co. also began the bottling of carbonated flavored sodas such as ginger ale by 1914, if not earlier. According to a 1921 Maine Agricultural Experient Station report, other flavors included Sarsaparilla, Lemon, Strawberry, and (imitation) Champagne Cider. At some point the company adopted "Hi-Brow" as a brand name and in the 1920s also produced offerings such as Hi-Brow Ginger Champagne, Hi-Brow Blood-Orange, and Hi-Brow Root Beer.

The original bottling operations at Granite State Spring Water were extensive and product distribution may have included prominent customers such as major league ball parks in Boston and elsewhere. Sales and distribution activities were robust enough to warrant a rail spur that came off of the Boston & Maine main line from the Westville section of town north of the bottling plant. The original plant was destroyed by fire in December 1922, despite the efforts of firefighter from at least five towns, including Portsmouth and Salem.

The company's bottling and distribution operations were quickly rebuilt after the disastrous fire, and in 1928 the enterprise was reincorporated as Old Hampshire, Inc. (with Wentworth serving as its President for at least the first few years). The Hi-Brow branding continued as well as a Mar-Vo line of soft beverages. Surviving bottle caps from this era reflect unique flavors such as Grape Ade, Cream Soda, Birch Beer, Cocoa Cream as well as an Old Hampshire Dry. The earlier sale of bottled spring water was apparently not continued into the 1920s, presumably because the carbonated flavored soft drinks were simply more profitable.

The Old Hampshire operations were purchased by C. Leary & Company in 1940 or 1941. In addition to a Leary line of flavors (Golden Ginger Ale, Imitation Grape and Old Fashion Root Beer), the plant bottled the NuGrape brand and eventually 7Up's line of carbonated beverages. Operations at 11

Wentworth Avenue ceased about 1970, but the front portions of the main building survive today as the bus terminal for a charter motor carrier company. The building's pediment still proudly proclaims its origins for all to see: "1911 Granite State Spring Water Company."

POISED FOR THE POST WAR BOOM

Many of New Hampshire's water and soft drink bottling firms did not fare well throughout the challenges of the Great Depression and the severe supply shortages of the World War II years. But other Granite State concerns were steadily gaining ground and positioning themselves to serve the burgeoning Baby Boom generation—a very thirsty generation as we'll see in Chapters 5 and 6.

5 THE HEYDAYS OF FIZZ: 1950-2000

> In 1900 the average annual per-employee output of bottled soft drink was 4,400 cases. By the mid-1950s mechanization and automation had pushed that number to over 26,000 cases.
> Source: Riley, 1972.

At the start of the 1950s, the United States was firmly positioned to skyrocket into economic prosperity, coupled with increased opportunities for the middle class to enjoy extended leisure times and family travel. The country started the decade with 6,662 soda bottling plants providing an almost untold numbers of brands and individual flavors. The most popular flavors overall reported for 1954 were:[67]

Cola/Kola	64%
Orange	6%
Lemon, Lime & Lemon-Lime	9%
Root Beer & Sarsaparilla	4%
Ginger Ale	4%
Grape	2%
Carbonated Waters/Club Soda	2%
All Other Flavors	9%

For carbonated soda, size matters, and segmented marketing data reveal interesting trends and socially-driven behaviors. The so-called Flavor Sales Ratios used in the beverage industry demonstrate how flavors vary with container size and the content's ultimate purpose. Perhaps the most striking example of this segmentation is seen in the Ginger Ale and the Carbonated Waters/Club Soda categories. Together those two flavors captured a whopping 46% of the large-container carbonated soda market (defined as 28 to 32-ounce bottles, the largest containers available to consumers at that time). Their dominance in the "big bottle" segment is likely due to the extensive use of these flavors as mixers for the myriad of alcoholic beverages popular during that 1950s era. A different picture emerges when examining the category of single-serve bottles (containing a mere six to seven ounces of beverage, the normal portion for that era). In that category, the Ginger Ale and Club Soda beverages together only accounted for 3% of total soda sales.

Number of NH bottling plants that at one time or another produced:

Crush 11
7Up 8
Wink 1
Grape soda (all brands) 23
Strawberry (all brands) 30
Root Beer (all brands) 41
Ginger ale (all brands) 48
Source: Fewless & Weide, 2014.

> In the 1930s both an increase in market opportunities and long-distance distribution challenges led soft drink bottlers to move away from a single central plant model. They adopted a franchise approach with localized product distribution, a model that remains to this day. This development benefited many New Hampshire bottlers that could continue to produce their own beverage lines but also bottle and distribute more national brands.
> Source: Riley, 1972.

Several critical trends were developing at this start to the second half of the century that would shape the industry itself, and in turn, consumer habits and preferences. One notable trend was rising prices. At the 32nd annual convention of American Bottles of Carbonated Beverages held in November 1950, the demise of the five-cent soda was forecasted. "It is only a matter of time – a very short time – until the last of the 5-cent drinks will only be a memory." That same year bottlers were fretting over increased costs coupled with material shortages and freight issues. Sugar shortages and price hikes had raised their ugly head once again. Manufacturers and distributors of all types were complaining there weren't enough railroad box cars to meet the rapidly-growing consumer demands, and that was threatening to slow down the economy. (This seems eerily reminiscent of the 2020-2023 supply-chain woes caused by the COVID-19 pandemic disruptions.)

> What was the life span of a typical returnable soda bottle? About 4 to 6 years, which meant an average of 30 to 35 fill/refill cycles.
> Source: Jacobs, 1959.

In 1948 glass manufacturers introduced lighter weight beverage bottles to the beer and soft drink industries that were also engineered to contain the pressures of carbonation. The non-returnable or "one-trip" bottle meant that stores and distributors would no longer need to handle and sort "empties." It also meant that bottlers could better concentrate on product fulfillment activities and avoid the chore of inspecting and cleaning those empties. In the late 1940s returnable bottles could have a lifespan of as few as two dozen re-fills to begin with, so they were certainly not everlasting (although the reuse cycles of returnable bottles were kinder to the environment than the single-use containers).

Non-returnable bottles were not exactly a new idea. Canada Dry had experimented with them starting in 1931 but dropped the practice after a few years due to cost. The extra cost factor was still present in 1950 and served to slow any adoption of one-way bottles.[68] However, practices do change, especially when driven by evolving consumer preferences for convenience. Virtually 100% of commercial soft drink products in the U.S. were produced in returnable (reusable) bottles in the late 1940s. But fifty years later less than 1% of all carbonated soda products could be purchased in returnable containers.

As with the non-returnable bottle, carbonated soda in cans experienced a similar slow adoption in the post-war years. Can manufacturers had largely solved the problem of seam leakage and product-caused corrosion of the metal container. Starting with Clicquot Club's mid-1930s experiment, some cone-top cans found a niche in the marketplace, but primarily the flat-top cans prevailed (easier to stack in shipment and took less shelf space at the retailer). But as with the non-returnable bottles, the one-way cans increased the bottler's costs, and this was a major reason in slowing their market penetration. However, beverages in cans were ideal for overseas orders, and many brands used them for shipments to military installations.

Another post-war trend was the development of the artificial sweetener calcium cyclamate and sodium cyclamate for soft drinks in 1952-53.

Sugarless beverages became popular primarily for diabetics, rather than initially as "diet" drinks for calorie-conscience consumers. Prominent market positions were won by Nehi /Royal Crown with their "Diet-Rite" brand; the Cott Beverage Corp. of New Haven, CT; and especially Kirsch Beverages, Inc. of Brooklyn, NY with their "No-Cal" line. By 1957 annual industry sales reached approximately five million cases and climbed steadily from there, the category's success surprising even many beverage industry executives.

In 1962 Diet Moxie was introduced as was Dietetic Dr Pepper, soon to be renamed just Diet Dr Pepper. During that developing era, Coca-Cola was reluctant to put its storied name on a diet drink, and so explored four-letter names that would catch the consuming public's attention. The company's marketing group first settled on TABB, but then shortened it to a stylized TaB. The new offering was a rapid success, soon out pacing rival Diet-Rite in sales. Coke tried a variety of TaB favor offerings but, when all was said and done, it was the cola flavor that took hold with the all-important consumer. However, a differently-marketed diet Coke product, grapefruit-flavored Fresca, launched in 1966 and did prove to have staying power with the consumer.

The post-World War II period witnessed another shift in America's beverage habits–a decline in soda fountain sales of carbonated soft drinks. Certainly, the growing population also had a growing appetite for soft drinks, but several factors were at play contributing to this shift in commerce. Soda fountains' forte was the single-serve beverage, with or without ice cream, and that required hand-crafting by a trained counter attendant.

Figure 12 The Squog Fruit and Ice Cream Bar was located in Granite Square, West Manchester. In this undated photo Chris Toli is behind the counter ready to serve thirsty customers. The store was forced to close in May 1983 due to a wide-scale urban renewal project. Credit: Manchester Historic Association.

As families moved out of urban areas to the suburbs, and fast-food restaurants and self-service convenient store offerings became prevalent, patronage at the pharmacy or five-and-ten cents store declined. After the war, more American families purchased a variety of household appliances, including electric refrigerators. Taking home bottled or canned soft drinks from the expanding chain of efficient supermarkets became the norm for suburban families. Even those products saw increased competition from the ready-mix flavored syrup concentrates like Za-Rex (started in 1912 in South Boston), the convenient packets of powdered Kool-Aid, and even the single-serving pill-in-foil novelty of Fizzies. The grocery chains were eager to promote these alternatives to bottled beverages in part because of their space-saving benefits—more profits per foot of precious shelf space. The old-fashion soda fountain wasn't yet on the road to extinction thanks to its partial adaptation in suburban settings. However, its best fountain sales days were in the past.

Illustration 11 Fizzies were created in 1957 by the Emerson Drug Co., makers of Bromo-Seltzer. With the addition of some flavoring, they marketed the tablets as convenient instant drinks – and no bottles to return to the store!

One additional trend in the second half of the 20th century is worth noting–the franchising of major brands. The franchising of soft drinks was certainly not unique to the 1950s; many local bottlers had adapted to producing both their own line of flavored products at the same time that they bottled and distribute one or more regional or national brands. But as the chain supermarkets grew at the expense of the corner store, increasingly they tended to stock those bottled beverages that were most widely known to the consumer through national advertising campaigns. Smaller and lesser-known brands often found they were fighting a losing battle for shelf space in the very venues that American families were increasingly favoring. Each year after the mid-century mark saw fewer and fewer independent and smaller soda bottlers remaining viable in the soft drink marketplace.

A 1956 soft drink advertising campaign developed the slogan, "Life is great....when you carbonate!" Another campaign from the 1970s coined the phrase, "Think of it (soda) as exciting water!"
Source: Lofland, 1986.

THE NEW HAMPSHIRE SCENE

New Hampshire was able to claim some twenty-five different operational soft drink bottling plants in 1954, a number proportionate to the size and population of the Granite State given the times, and a mere 554,000 residents. Understandably, more populated sister states, such as Massachusetts, could boast six times that number of bottlers within their state borders. The beverage industry experienced nationwide growth in the post-World War II years, but the associated innovation and necessary adaptation was a severe challenge for the smaller enterprises. New Hampshire's primarily family-run operations with their neighborhood customer base were seeing increased pressures from competitors and the forces of economy-of-scale. In 1954 only seven of the State's twenty-five bottlers could count a workforce numbering twenty or more employers. The next few decades would bring signification consolidation and attrition within the soft beverage industry, and New Hampshire was affected by this national tide. The following sections take a closer look at four home-grown firms that made a sizeable impact on the State's soft drink marketplace: Lafayette Beverages of Derry and Manchester, Cott Beverages of Manchester, Cocheco Bottling of Rochester, and Nashua's Lucky Strike Ginger Ale.

* * *

LAFAYETTE BEVERAGES, DERRY AND MANCHESTER

Lafayette Beverages (and all its ownership and name permutations) may hold one of the longest and perhaps most storied profiles of any New Hampshire soft drink bottler. It all started with a natural spring in West Derry on the road to Windham and an 1825 visit by the great Revolutionary War general, the Marquis de Lafayette. While visiting and dining in Derry, the General was provided drinking water collected from Crystal Spring and was duly impressed with its taste and purity—so much so that it is reported Lafayette requested two barrels be sent to his Boston hotel for his later enjoyment.[69]

The Crystal Spring site itself was unimpressive by any standard–a small hole in the ground surrounded by an oak tub where locals could help themselves to a cool drink. A chemist who tested the spring water in 1882 declared it to be of unique composition, something worth protecting and charging for[70]. The land owner quickly responded to the report by constructing a brick cistern at the spring site and began selling its water to all takers under the name Derry Mineral Spring Water. In 1891 he sold his money-making spring for $1,500 to a group of investors that included the original chemist and two Derry businessmen, Greenleaf Bartlett and

Frederick Shepard. Colonel Shepard was a well-established banker in town and would also become prominent in public service. But his greatest claim to fame in modern eyes may be that he was the grandfather to Derry's future famous test pilot and our country's first astronaut, Alan B. Shepard.

The new investors formed and trademarked the Lafayette Mineral Spring Company. They greatly improved the site with the construction of an elaborate structure and began selling water locally for five cents a gallon. This seemed to be a decent price for a drink that not only tasted great but (as claimed) would "cure constipation and headache." However, at some point Col. Shepard and his investors determined that the spring water business was not for them. One report claims they were swindled by a salesman who worked for them and, discouraged with overall low profits, eagerly sold the business to an Ernst L. Abbott[71].

Abbott kept the business in Derry and ran it successfully for some twenty years at various locations in town[72] before his son Howard took over the helm from 1910 until the end of World War II. During this period, like so many other bottlers and distributors of the time, the Abbotts branched out from just selling raw spring water to also offering flavored carbonated beverages.

Clear glass bottles with "LMS" embossed on the front can be found by collectors today, as well as paper-labeled bottles touting the "Nutfield" brand. Nutfield was the original designation for towns now known as Derry, Londonderry and parts of Hampstead and Windham. During this period, the Lafayette Mineral Spring Co. was known to have produced several Nutfield-branded flavors, including Blood Orange Tonic, Root Beer, Ginger Ale, and Strawberry Tonic. Evidence indicates the Abbotts also controlled a Moxie distributorship during this same period.

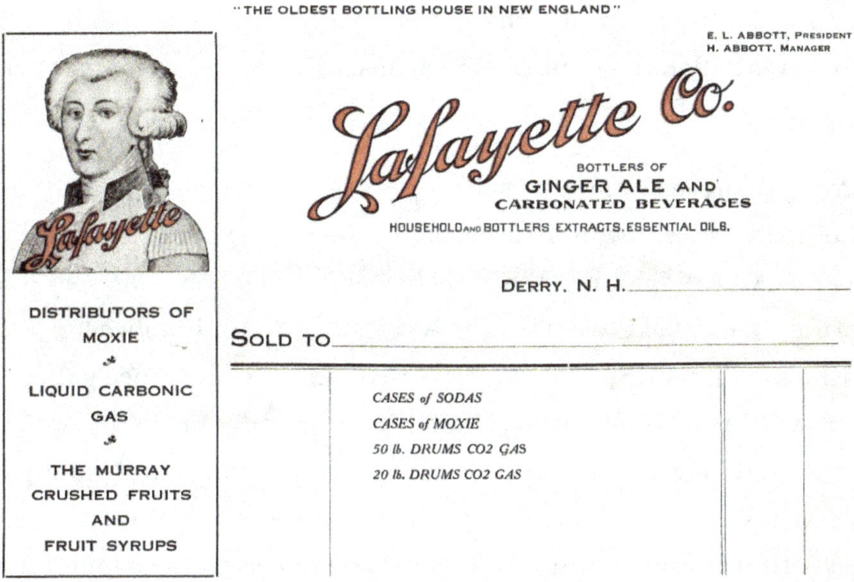

"THE OLDEST BOTTLING HOUSE IN NEW ENGLAND"

E. L. ABBOTT, President
H. ABBOTT, Manager

Lafayette Co.

BOTTLERS OF
GINGER ALE AND
CARBONATED BEVERAGES
HOUSEHOLD AND BOTTLERS EXTRACTS, ESSENTIAL OILS.

DERRY. N. H.

SOLD TO

DISTRIBUTORS OF

MOXIE

LIQUID CARBONIC GAS

THE MURRAY CRUSHED FRUITS AND FRUIT SYRUPS

CASES of SODAS
CASES of MOXIE
50 lb. DRUMS CO2 GAS
20 lb. DRUMS CO2 GAS

Figure 13 Lafayette Co. letterhead (ca. 1900) when still owned by Ernst L. Abbott of Derry. Note the distribution of Moxie as well as syrups and crushed fruits – commonly used by soda fountains to create flavored counter drinks. Credit: Marc Jolicoeur.

Faced with growing competition from national brands and larger bottlers, Lafayette Mineral Spring Co. closed its doors in the early 1920s, with legal dissolution occurring in April 1925. Around this time, the rights to the bottling operations and the spring were assumed by Adelard D. LeMay of Manchester, who may have continued the Derry business for a few years at a Railroad Avenue location under the name Lafayette Bottling Company. But Derry was still a relatively rural community at the time, and LeMay reasoned that the abundance of fellow Franco-Americans in Manchester could provide an expanded customer base. He relocated the bottling operations to a compact 700 square-foot building on Harvard Street on the east side of

Manchester. The Lafayette Spring itself was sold and more or less left to return to its natural state by the 1930s. In 1993 the once-notable Derry landmark was bulldozed as part of an expansive housing development in the area.

LeMay achieved modest success with increasing demand from neighborhood store owners, especially French-Canadian storekeepers. However, LeMay did not run the Manchester soda business for very long.[73] On April 1, 1926, a bakery delivery driver named Antonio Jolicoeur bought the bottling plant with $500 down, borrowed on a life insurance policy, and 16 years' worth of monthly payments, for a grand sum of $3,800. This transaction left Jolicoeur, a man with a young and growing family to support, with 43 cents cash, a small inventory of beverages and an unfailing desire to succeed with this new venture. Few would have guessed the beginning of a new era that would position Lafayette Bottling Company as a major player in the soft drink marketplace until well into the 1980s.

Jolicoeur was not a man to let grass grow under his feet and had no intention of failing at his new business venture. One of his very first sales calls was to a Pearl Street variety store operated by his former boarding house landlady, whom he knew had a penchant for purchasing goods for her shelves in cash. Jolicoeur made a cash sale and never looked back from there; even when the typical challenges of a retail business rose to test his resolve. He had been in business only six months when beverage companies came under regulation by the State Department of Health, and he was ordered to install a new bottle washer at a cost of $2,600—funds he did not have at the time. Unthwarted, Jolicoeur somehow talked the Liquid Carbonic Company into providing him with one of their washers on a three-year note. Crisis averted.

Layfette Bottling turned the financial corner in 1931 when increasing sales allowed them to move to a larger, more efficient facility on the corner of Wilson and Somerville Streets in Manchester. They were still very much a minor league player in the soft drink industry; however, growth was steady, even with the challenges posed by the Great Depression.

Figure 14 A production room at Lafayette Bottling ca. 1931. Owner Antonio Jolicoeur (straw hat) is accompanied by two employees. The product surrounding them is 28 oz. ginger ale. Credit: Marc Jolicoeur.

In 1936 Jolicoeur decided to join forces with Pepsi-Cola in a marriage that even he thought would not pan out. He was so pessimistic about the business collaboration that at first he refused to purchase a $315 unit of concentrate from Pepsi in order to bottle the cola beverage. Instead, Jolicoeur purchased 100 cases of Pepsi-Cola from a Lynn, Massachusetts bottler to first test the waters among his Manchester customer base. Only after determining that his clientele really did like this cola drink did he commit to purchasing a unit of the concentrate – but not the extra $15 for a labeling attachment to accommodate the new 12-ounce bottles. That's what 11-year-old sons were for, and young Robert Jolicoeur was pressed into service with labels, a quart jar of glue, and a brush.

Figure 15 The Lafayette Bottling delivery fleet in Manchester, NH ca. 1940. They joined forces with Pepsi starting in 1936. Credit: Marc Jolicoeur.

Of course, as sales of Pepsi-Cola grew, the need for automated labeling became quite apparent, and even father Antonio relented. Young Robert also had a head for numbers and began to keep records of their sales of the Pepsi products. Through his own hand-written ledgers, he documented sales of 1,564 cases in 1936 rising to 172,467 cases in 1947, the only dip occurring during the World War II sugar rationing that limited production of all soft drink bottlers nationwide.

In 1941 the soft drink production operations were moved to even larger quarters at 305 Massabesic Street in Manchester, and the company name was changed to the Lafayette Beverage Company. Robert assumed operational control from his father in 1956, a period when the company offered a prolific line of bottled soft beverages. In addition to Pepsi products, the enterprise offered its New Hampshire customers Orange Kist, 7Up, Dr Pepper, Uptown, Frostie Old Fashion Root Beer, Lemmy Lemonade, Moxie, and its own Lafayette Ginger Ale. The ginger ale was generally sold in 28-ounce bottles and was one of the company's primary products during the 1920s up through the early 1940s, but they later also sold Schweppes Ginger Ale and Tonic water, consistent with most Pepsi bottlers. Moxie was a strong seller, especially through the 1950s, with about half-a-million cases sold annually[74].

In 1926 — Mr. Antonio Jolicoeur bought Lafayette Beverages —a small plant on Harvard Street and operated it as a one-man business.

In 1936—Lafayette Beverages, Inc. obtained the PEPSI COLA franchise, and since then has become distributor for MOXIE, KIST, FROSTIE OLD FASHION ROOT BEER AND LEMMY.

Now — in much expanded quarters at 305 Massabesic St., Mr. Jolicoeur and his sons, head a shop of forty-five employees and fifteen trucks servicing more than 2800 Lafayette accounts throughout the state.

Illustration 12 Lafayette Beverages was highlighted in the 1955 booklet, *"Manchester the Queen City."* Credit: The Manchester (NH) Chamber of Commerce.

Originally and through the 1970s, Lafayette's customer base was dispersed with no single giant account. "Grocers were grocers," as Marc Jolicoeur, Robert's son, has expressed, indicating a myriad of disseminated smaller accounts reflecting the retail landscape of the times. When supermarket chains became established, everything changed for the soft drink industry–as it did for cereal, soup, paper goods, and most all similar product lines.

Marc Jolicoeur[75] assumed primary responsibility for running the firm's Massabesic Street-based operations from his father in 1970. Layfette's relationship with Pepsi Cola continued to grow, and by the 1970s the Manchester operation was busy turning out over a million cases of Pepsi products each year. Pepsi produced the concentrate and contracted with bottlers to provide the sugar and water and bottle the final product. Sugar prices spiked in 1972, going from 10 cents a pound to over a dollar a pound that year, challenging the profits of bottlers like Lafayette. Soft drink giants like Coca-Cola had a distinct advantage over others since they produced their own syrup and were extremely savvy at navigating the global sugar market.

The 1970s also saw the increasing dominance of the non-returnable bottle and, by the mid-1980s, Lafayette offered its customers only one-way bottles. One of the greatest advantages of switching to non-returnable bottles from a bottler's perspective was the sanitation factor since brand-new bottles were the only containers utilized. One-way bottles virtually eliminated the previously constant stream of false claims that adulterated products had reached the retail shelves from improperly cleaned reusable bottles. Jolicoeur stressed that quality problems at the bottling operations constituted the primary reason a franchise could be threatened with cancelation or revocation by a major brand[76]. Even raw water purchased from the municipality required careful attention at the bottling plant since summer temperatures could bring deteriorated water quality. Unwanted taste, odors and even algae could raise havoc with the standard filtration systems and require the plant to employee additional quality control measures to purify the water before its use in the bottling process.

Speaking of water, the reader might naturally wonder if Lafayette Beverages ever bottled spring water for sale following the example of its Derry originators? Marc Jolicoeur laughed at this question and recalled how a Canadian salesman once tried to sell them on that very idea in the 1970s. Lafayette's response was something along the lines of, "Are you crazy? We're in New Hampshire. Who would pay for bottled water?" Thus, no bottled water products were offered for sale by Lafayette Beverages.

The 1980s brought continued change to Lafayette Beverages, and all other New Hampshire soft drink bottlers. To meet an expanding marketplace in New England and the challenges of modernizing an old-line business, Marc Jolicoeur oversaw the development of a new bottling facility in Ayer, Massachusetts, they called CPF, Inc. (for Central Processing Facility). CPF opened on April 8, 1983, and was followed by a sister facility for canned PepsiCo products. The canning facility was named EPIC Enterprises, which Pepsi officially claims stands for "Enjoy Pepsi in Cans." However, Marc who personally spearheaded this business expansion, is fond of saying that EPIC stood for "Every Purchase Includes a Check!" Those two central Massachusetts beverage processing facilities remain fully functional, thriving Pepsi operations to this day. Lafayette sold its storied Massabesic Street facility and opened a warehouse operation in a Manchester industrial park on what is now called Pepsi Road.

Lafayette Beverages sold its operations to PepsiCo in 1986. Although not the direction they wanted to take, the entire franchise system was changing, and this proved to be the most realistic path forward. A fifty-year successful run had come to a conclusion. The Dr Pepper and Moxie accounts couldn't remain in the fold and were spun off and picked up by Coca-Cola of Northern New England (CCNNE) operation out of Londonderry, New Hampshire (more about this entity in Chapter 6).

Figure 16 Wooden soda bottle crates like this one are popular with today's collectors.

* * *

COTT BEVERAGE CORPORATION, MANCHESTER

Similar to the story of Lafayette Beverages, the Cott Beverage Corporation also had a long and fairly complex history. Established in 1923 in Port Chester, New York, by Polish immigrant Solomon Cott and his son Harry, their hallmark was producing carbonated soft drinks that exhibited striking flavors. Branded as Cott Nectar Beverages, vibrant flavors were combined with global ingredients such as ginger from Jamaica, orange juice from California, lemons from Sicily, and raspberries from Oregon. This took place at a time when many soft drink producers leaned heavily on artificial flavors for their economy and ease of use.

The first few decades of operations brought popular Cott offerings including Orange, Cherry, Pale Dry Ginger Ale, Golden Ginger Ale, Club Soda, Tom Collins, Grape, Cola, Cream, Lemon-lime, Raspberry, Root Beer and Sarsaparilla[77]. Cott bottle caps indicated the flavor of the bottles' contents and caps are known to collectors for numerous additional flavors such as Sparkling Coffee, Apple Ginger, Birch Beer, Bitter Lemon, Black Cherry Punch, Cherry Cola, Cherry Strawberry, Chocolate Cream, Concord Punch, and many others. The company made its mark with the consuming public in the Northeast states with the winning combination of high quality and variety to satisfy a wide array of personal tastes. The company developed the memorable tag line used widely in its print advertising and signage: "It's Cott to be Good!"

Figure 17 Typical of 1950 and 1960s advertising, Cott Beverages advertisements often showcased a leisure-time setting for consuming their bottled beverages.

Cott operated a number of bottling plants in the Northeast, New Haven, Connecticut, being one of the largest and the one that seemed to serve as home base. The Manchester, New Hampshire, operations commenced with a partnership with Silver Brothers Company, a well-established, well-run wholesale grocery business (in fact, the largest such enterprise north of Boston). In 1948 the Silver Brothers (Henry and Morris) established a bottling plant at Mill 8 South in the Manchester Millyard (177 Granite Street) with new equipment to take advantage of their already-extensive food distribution system. Within six years of startup, this Cott plant was producing some eight million cases of beverage a year to satisfy its thirsty mid-century customers.[78]

Figure 18 In addition to its own line of sodas, for a period of time American Dry bottled for Moxie in Boston and for Cott in Manchester, NH. Clicquot Club experimented with cans in the 1930s but they didn't see wide acceptance for carbonated sodas until 1953.

The Cott corporation developed a major connection to the Canadian marketplace in 1952 when a Montreal clothier, Harry Pencer, sent his three sons to summer camp on Lake Winnipesaukee[79]. All three boys developed a fondness for Cott soda and its "17 heavenly delicious flavors" while at camp. Observing this, Pencer jumped on the business opportunity and made arrangements to import the beverage into the province of Quebec, where it proved to be quite popular. In 1955 he purchased the Stewart Bottling Company and secured the rights to produce Cott beverages in his newly-acquired plant. Over the next twenty years Pencer's company was able to establish province-wide brand loyalty for his products, even expanding his distribution to some of the other Canadian provinces and also back into the United States.

Another uniqueness of the Cott Beverage brand was their early embracing of low-calorie or dietetic bottled soft drinks. In 1949 a diet soda called La Casera was produced in Madrid, Spain (and is still available). The story of such beverages in the United States involved a Russian immigrant, Hyman Kirsch, who came to Brooklyn, New York, in 1903 and began to produce a ginger ale and other carbonated flavors. In the early 1950s Hyman and his son Morris were directors of the Jewish Sanitarium for Chronic Disease and wanted a sugar-free soft drink for the sanitarium's diabetic and cardiovascular patients. They directed their own beverage laboratories to search for a suitable sugar substitute and settled on calcium cyclamate. The Kirsch No-Cal Ginger Ale was introduced to the New York public in March 1953 with counter sales aimed primarily at diabetics. However, surveys revealed that at least half of the buyers were not diabetics but were individuals concerned with sugar and calories. The No-Cal line was then heavily promoted and the Ginger Ale joined by seven other flavor offerings developed by Kirsch Beverages.[80]

Noting the success of Kirsch in this new-found beverage marketplace, Cott Beverages lost no time in fully jumping into the race as a May 22, 1953 display ad in the *Washington Post* indicates:

> Now available...non-fattening in six naturally wonderful flavors. Not one bit fattening!... That's Cott Sugar-Free beverages! You know Cott quality, from Cott beverages with sugar...No fear of adding weight, or breaking your diet. Cott quality may cost a little more, but you know why at first TASTE. Now—enjoy yourself, with these delicious new dietetic treats.

Cott initially branded its diet beverage line as "Cott Low Calorie, Non-Fatting," but would later shift to using "Sugar Free Cott Quality Diet" on its container labels. The company produced its line of diet offerings from New Haven as well as several of the satellite plants, including Manchester, New Hampshire.

The Manchester and New Haven plants later developed yet another line of diet sodas under the brand name Metri Cola. Like Kirsch's No-Cal, Metri Cola had its roots in concerns for human health. Mead Johnson and Company was built on science-based nutrition by Edward Mead Johnson Sr. who previously had co-founded Johnson & Johnson with his brother. One of their more well-known products was their 1961 creation of Pablum for infant nutrition. In June 1961 they also patented a sugar-free beverage they called Metri Cola. The Metri-Cola Beverage Company was formed in association with American Dry Beverage Corp of Manchester – an affiliation of Cott Beverages. "Low Calorie Metri Cola, The Diet Cola" was widely sold in dark green one-quart glass bottles through the extensive Cott/Silver Brothers distribution network.

Figure 19 This diet soda, originally developed for health management, was widely sold by Cott Beverages of Manchester.

Other beverage companies rushed into the diet soda marketplace as well—some faster than others. In 1954 Canada Dry launched a ginger ale called Glamor that was targeted toward women. Royal Crown/Nehi first introduced Diet Rite Cola in 1953, and after some formula adjustments, they began to market the beverage in earnest several years later. By 1962 it was the fourth best-selling cola in the country behind regular Coke, Pepsi and its own RC Cola. Other brands were astounded at this success and motivate to compete. Moxie offered the consuming public Diet Moxie, and Dr Pepper developed Dietetic Dr Pepper in 1962. They were shortly joined by offerings from the industry giants with Coca-Cola's TaB in 1963 and Pepsi's Patio Diet Cola in 1964.

What was it like to work at Cott Beverages during the company's peak years of operation? Evangelos "Van" Demetriades worked for Cott in Manchester during the summers of 1956 to 1960 while he was attending college. As a summer employee he was often called upon for many fill-in tasks wherever additional hands were needed. Invariable, there was a great deal of hard physical labor involved, partially the consequence of operating a bottling facility in a multi-story former textile mill in Manchester's Millyard. Some of the hard labor tasks for summer employees resulted from the site's foreman awarding the easiest jobs to his favorite regular workers.[81]

Van would often be assigned to unload freight cars containing new glass bottles that had to be transported and stored three floors up until needed by the bottlers. Glass bottles were stored sorted by colors – clear for most flavors but green bottles for ginger ale. During these years all of Cott's bottles were the durable returnables as the one-way bottles were still not in wide use by most bottling companies. One of his least favorite tasks was being assigned to load the empties returned from the stores into the bottle washing and sterilization equipment. The bottles all had to be inspected and were often returned to the plant filthy. (Although to Van's very pleasant surprise, one night when he was drearily feeding the soaker machine, he found a rolled up twenty-dollar bill in one of the returned bottles!)

Over the multiple summers that he worked for Cott, Van would be assigned to one of the bottling lines. Typically, he worked a 6:00 PM to 6:00 AM shift each week and then continue until noon on Saturday, earning a welcomed twenty-five hours of overtime pay each week. The plant was filling product in 7-ounce, 12-ounce and quart glass bottles as well as 12-ounce cans. Problems would arise that slowed down or even stopped the machinery. Glass would break and necessitate stoppage to reset the line. Labels wouldn't stick properly to the bottles after filling. It was indeed a busy, sometimes chaotic place, especially with the high summer demand for refreshing soft drinks, and so workers felt the constant pressure to get product out the door.

As with virtually any type of production or manufacturing activity with its associated demands and pressures, sometimes mistakes were made. One night Van was on a bottling crew filling 7-ounce bottles with Half & Half soda. Around midnight after having bottled several hundred 30-bottle cases, one of the owners came into the bottling room and looked up at the clear hose that connected the syrup room on the floor above to the bottling line. The owner realized immediately that the color of the mixture was incorrect and raced up to the syrup room in an agitated state where he fired the night chemist on the spot. Van and the bottling crew spent the rest of that evening uncapping and emptying all the bottles they had just filled so they could be rewashed and refilled on the next shift.

The Cott Bottling Company's demise reflects a somewhat convoluted picture in several respects. In 1962 Clicquot Club Beverages became part of the Cott family, adding their Millis, Massachusetts bottling operation to the fold. But in 1967 Henry Silver sold his interest in the soft drink company to National Industries, Inc. of Kentucky to focus his attention on his alcoholic beverage distributorship. Cott was operated as a wholly-owned subsidiary of National Industries for a period of time. But at some point, Cott ceased bottling and distributing their soft drink products and turned to supplying concentrate to contract bottlers, much in the fashion that the Moxie Company had done in the early 1950s. In 1971 they reportedly were suppling concentrate to over 100 contract bottlers. Various ownership changes occurred over the next decades, and in 2019 Cott Corporation, now headquartered in Tampa, Florida, exited the soft drink concentrate market entirely. Rebranded as Primo Water Corporation, the company now focuses on the residential and commercial water service market, having left the flavored soft drinks far behind.

What was the fate of the Manchester bottling plant that served Cott Beverages to loyal New Hampshire customers for so many years? It is unclear exactly when soft drink bottling or concentrate production ceased at Mill 8 South, but the remaining Silver Brothers distribution operation vacated the building in 1976, moving to a newly-constructed facility near the Manchester airport. Much of the former textile building was demolished later that year, partly as a component of a millyard revitalization initiative, and also to allow for a major lane widening project along the expanding Granite Street thoroughfare.

I frequently photographed the changes in the Manchester Millyard during those years of revitalization and change. When the former Cott/Silver Brothers structure was in the process of being demolished, one quiet Saturday morning the site supervisor allowed me access to pursue my photographic endeavors. Equipment, furniture and most everything else had been removed from the building's interior spaces. However, one of the rooms that I came across had apparently been used to store and distribute Cott promotional materials, some of which were still present in scattered, broken boxes. Sadly, all of the room's contents were slated to become part of the wrecking ball's debris field to be hauled away for disposal. In the mid-1970s, Cott memorabilia was not of particular interest to most soft drink collectors who typically were focused on the top brands like Coca-Cola. Before leaving Mill 8 South I gathered up a few plastic pens, a few pocket protectors and a 5-inch round sticker with red lettering advertising "Cott Quality Beverages only 5¢, 7 Oz. Bottles." That tattered paper sticker is my only remaining keepsake from the dismantling of this once expansive and successful New Hampshire soft drink giant.

Illustration 13 This round price sticker represents the last item rescued from the former Cott bottling plant in the Manchester Millyard. The vacated building at Mill 8 South was demolished in 1976.

* * *

COCHECO BOTTLING COMPANY, ROCHESTER

As with so many other soft drink bottlers at the turn of the 20th century, the Cocheco Bottling Company's roots were of the pharmaceutical persuasion. Eugene W. Emerson was a well-known and well-respected druggist in Rochester, New Hampshire. He had previously worked at the drug store of his maternal uncle and eventually co-owned and ran drug stores in Farmington and Hillsboro, New Hampshire, before establishing himself in Rochester around 1890. We know that the Farmington store contained a soda fountain, and by 1895 (possibly as early as 1890 according to company advertising) Emerson had established Emerson & Company bottlers on Summer Street in Rochester. This bottling venture was quite likely in addition to, or possibly even an adjunct to, his core pharmacy business. In an advertisement of the day, his enterprise claimed, "Manufacturers of Mineral and Soda Waters, and general bottlers." We don't know many of the specifics regarding his product lines but both clear and aqua blob-top Emerson bottles with attractive embossed script are known to collectors today.[82]

Emerson sold his Rochester bottling business in March 1904 to three Lucey brothers, James E. Jr., David J. and John F. who rebranded the enterprise as the Cocheco Bottling Works. Cocheco is an Abenaki word for "rapid foaming waters," and the Cocheco River is a prominent landmark running through the towns of Farmington, Rochester, and Dover. Numerous organizations have incorporated the name into their identifier over the years. Under the Luceys' proprietorship, the bottling works was known to produce ginger ale, tonic water, as well as orange and lemon-lime sodas.

In 1917 the Lucey brothers sold their business to Alfred Lagasse who began operating it with his sons, leading to a long period of success in the New Hampshire soft drink industry. Cocheco Bottling Works started out at the original Emerson & Company location on Summer Street but by late 1940s moved the operation to a larger facility on Lowell Street.

The 1940s were challenging for all food and beverage producers, soft drink concerns included. Rationing of all types during World War II necessitated many adjustments to most every facet of the business from rubber tires and gasoline for delivery trucks to many food ingredients. Sugar, a vital component of all non-dietetic beverages, was often in short supply both during the war years and for some periods afterwards. A 1942 newspaper article reported on production curtailments at Cocheco Botting due to a 40 percent reduction in its sugar allocation. Normally using sixty tons of sugar annually, Cocheco temporarily suspended production of its "cheaper grades of beverages" – presumably its own line of sodas rather than the national and regional brands that it bottled under contract.

Later in 1942 Cocheco Bottling filled its first order for the U.S. Army when it shipped 500 cases of orange soda to a base exchange in Boston to be sent to troops overseas. They claimed to be the first of New Hampshire's soft drink producers to provide such a designated shipment, with more to follow in 1,000 case increments.[83] A 1943 news article further explained that Cocheco was allotted quota-exempt sugar, bottle caps and other production materials to be able to fulfill these military shipments.

Company management was quoted in print musing over the practical problem of getting its empty bottles returned from far-flung overseas theaters of war. Once turned over to the military, it is highly unlikely that many, if any, of Cocheco's empty soda bottles ever found their way back to Rochester, New Hampshire to be refilled. The barriers were many, including reports of SeeBees (Naval Construction Battalions) adapting heavy glass soda bottles for use as electrical insulators in a pinch.

"Empties," as they were commonly called by the bottlers and the public alike, always presented a thorn-in-the-side of soft drink producers. War-time shortages and rationing just make the problem all that much worse, even within the domestic marketplace. In a December 1942 issue of the *Newmarket News*, Cocheco's large display ad touted the pleasures and energy pick-up advantages of its Orange Crush, but pleaded with the patriotic public to "Return Your Empty Bottles Today!"

> Yes, they are just empties – but each will soon be washed, sterilized and refilled with America's leading bottled soft drink – and be back in the lines again to help some thirsty American strike another effective blow at the Axis.

The host of activities revolving around returnable soda bottles wasn't limited to World War II conditions, of course. From the inception of bottle deposit fees, the exchange of empty hunks of heavy glass for cold, hard cash became a source of "found" money for millions of youngsters and adults alike. While growing up, I frequently harvested extra spending money through the collection and return of soda bottles scrounged from home or rescued from roadside discards. The sometimes mud-caked bottles would fetch either 2¢ (single serving) or a whopping 5¢ (quart size) at the friendly corner grocer. The neighborhood proprietor often provided a dose of unwarranted kindness by accepting bottles for brands he didn't even carry. It probably helped that he knew whatever coinage he turned over to us in exchange for our bag of empties he'd reclaim through our immediate purchase of a bottle of our favorite tonic–maybe also a Sky Bar or NECCO Wafers if our bottle collecting venture had gone well.

Long-time Manchester resident Patricia LeFrancois recalls collecting soda empties with her sister during their youth and storing them in a shed behind their house. With parents providing limited spending money in tight times, the sisters would use bottle redemption funds to pay for two tickets to a local movie theater's Saturday-afternoon show. In the winter the sisters would bundle up and make the trip to their backyard shed where cold hands would sort through the weeks' worth of collected bottles and tally up the expected payoff. If the count was enough for two tickets, the girls' movie outing would be a reality and their father would drive them with their bottles to the corner store to cash them in. If the count fell short, it meant more scouring of the neighborhood for additional empties while patiently waiting for the following weekend's entertainment opportunity. The sisters considered all of these youthful efforts to be great fun and kept fond memories into their adult years.[84]

One hallmark of the Cocheco Bottling Company, a modest-size operation by most measures, was the variety of products they produced and distributed over the decades. From 1948 to 1972 they had a Clicquot Club franchise and bottled all of that brand's flavors. But they also bottled Orange Crush, Squirt, Royal Crown, Nehi, and Moxie and had several lines of house beverages under the names Cheeco Beverages, Cocheco Club, Casco, and Jic-Jac. Cocheco Club flavors included popular mixers like Golden Ginger Ale, Sparkling Water, Tom Collins, Lime Ricky, but also kid-favorites such as Strawberry, Lemon-lime, and something they called Buzz (grapefruit based).

ROCHESTER...

Manufacturing center for

CLICQUOT BEVERAGES

throughout all

New Hampshire

•

- **21 Delicious Flavors**
- **Honest Full Quarts**
- **Regular or Sugar-Free**
- **Sold all over the World**

Cocheco Bottling Company

INC.

Rochester, New Hampshire

"64th Year Of Progress"

Illustration 14 This 1954 sales flyer from Cocheco Bottling Co. reflects the Clicquot Club franchise they held from 1948 to 1972.

The Jic-Jac line saw its heyday from 1962 to 1970 and its selling point was both non-returnable bottles and a lower price point. The company hyped both features in an April 22, 1964 *Portsmouth Herald* display advertisement stressing "the bottles you don't bring back." The ad also let the public in on a little beverage industry "secret" – that it was costly to produce "a complete line of rainbow flavors" and therefore Jic-Jac logically stuck to just the four that were most popular: Cola, Pale Dry (ginger ale), Orange and Root Beer.

Probably no single brand of carbonated soda could capture the attention of consumers and newspaper reporters like Moxie, and Cocheco Bottling Works was one of the largest bottlers of this dark liquid "ambrosia" in northern New England. From all accounts, Cocheco had a sixty- year relationship with Moxie starting with the 1917 purchase by Alfred Lagasse. As a brand, Moxie had its highs and lows and wasn't always a well-managed firm throughout its own 135- year storied history. However, Cocheco seemed to pair well with this quintessential New England soft drink, and the brand's most loyal following was located in their proverbial backyard: Maine, New Hampshire and Vermont. Because Moxie is "an acquired taste" and has been largely a regional seller, it has been assumed by many over the last five decades that Moxie has long-ago passed from the scene. But no, Moxie is still produced today and is actually the oldest continually-bottled soft drink in the country (more on that story in Chapter 6).

Illustration 15 Even venerable Moxie had switched to no-deposit, no-return bottles by the early 1960s. The Mad About Moxie tagline took advantage of generously free publicity provided to the firm by Mad Magazine.

Moxie's widely assumed demise was the subject of a November 11, 1973, article in the *New Hampshire Sunday News*: "Make No Mistake About This, Moxie Is Alive and Well Here." The newspaper article with its extensive photographs profiled Cocheco Bottling Company and its love affair and history of success selling Moxie. Herve Lagasse, Alfred's son, was running the bottling company and was extensively interviewed for the multi-page article. Lagasse stressed the importance of Moxie sales to his company, with over 300,000 cases a year produced and distributed in box trucks with the famous Moxie Man painted on its sides instructing, "Ya Gotta Have Moxie." To answer the question of Moxie's unique taste, Lagasse replied, "Moxie isn't a root beer and it isn't a cola. If you don't like it, well just don't buy it."

The Cocheco Bottling Company ceased business in 1977, and the structure where so many brands of soda were bottled for so many years is now the site of a building material supply business. Many individuals still recall the Cocheco operations with fond memories (as posted on social media):

> "I used to work there. The best Moxy (sic) was right off the line fresh." – T.M.

> "My father worked there for many years and I worked there as a kid." – L.W.

> "I lived across the street, we used to go buy soda for 10 cents." – F.M.

* * *

LUCKY STRIKE GINGER ALE COMPANY, NASHUA

Judging by favorable newspaper articles published over the decades, Lucky Strike Ginger Ale Company of Nashua was always a hometown favorite, even in a city with numerous soft drink bottlers. What is also clear is that Joseph W. Simoneau, who founded the firm in 1922 served as its constant and unabashed promoter every chance he had up until his passing in 1968.

Initially operating on Canal Street in the city, Lucky Strike moved to 308 Main Street in the early 1940s and eventually to 37 East Hollis Street in the 1970s. From the start the company considered its hallmark to be quality ingredients and a final bottled beverage offered to the grocers and the public at a very attractive price point compared to its competition. In an August 1943 article in the *Nashua Telegraph* newspaper, Simoneau emphasized the superiority of his new Grandma's Root Beer with its scientifically-blended eight herbs combined with the best wintergreen, hops, juniper berries, birch bark, sassafras and other ingredients. No doubt this was indeed a fine soft beverage as the owner touted in print, notwithstanding that these ingredients are common to almost any root beer recipe dating back to the mid-1800s.

Sales figures for Lucky Strike through the years are not available, but the Nashua bottler appears to have been its busiest during the 1950s and into the 1960s. The plant was equipped with modern bottling equipment purchased in 1949 that produced a hundred cases each hour and efficient bottle washing and sterilization equipment handled all the returned empties. Syrup, which was typically made from fresh fruit, was prepared on site in large stainless-steel tanks. The operation served grocers in five states, created syrup for other soft drink bottlers, and the public could order product directly from the Main Street plant if they wished. In addition to the company's namesake Ginger Ale and the Grandma's Root Beer, popular flavors included Concord Punch (from grapes), Lemon & Lime, Orange (with California oranges), and Slyng (with grapefruit).[85]

REG. IN UNITED STATES AND CANADIAN PAT. OFF.

Lucky Strike
GINGER ALE CO.

Nashua, N. H. _OCT 3_ 19_7_

Sold to _Temple St Superette_

Address __________

½ PTS.	PINTS	QUARTS	ARTICLE	PRICE	AMOUNT
		2	GINGER GOLDEN		5,00
1	4		PALE DRY		10,00
			SPARK. WATER		
1	2		ORANGE SUNKIST FLAVORED		5,00
	1		ROOT BEER (NEW)		2,50
			LEMON-LIME		
	1		STRAWBERRY WILD		2,50
3			119 mix		
1	1		CREAM SODA		2,50
			CHUM-COLA-NEW		
			CONCORD PUNCH		
			TOM COLLINS MIX		
6					9,60
			GRAPE FRUIT-LEMON		
			SLYNG - MIXER		
			FOUNTAIN SYRUP		
			CARBONIC GAS		
			TOTAL		37,10
			CREDIT-EMPTIES		12,50
					24,60

By Cash or Check __________

Goods Rec'd by __________

PHONES
TU. 2-0761 - 2-4364
39 East Hollis Street

THE POTTER-PRESS BOSTON

N 5969

Illustration 16 October 1967 Lucky Strike Ginger Ale sales representative's order form for the Temple Street Superette in Nashua. The neighborhood convenient store is still operating as the Temple Street Market. Note the credit for the "empties" (returned bottles).

By the 1970s the number of small grocers and mom and pop corner stores throughout New England had greatly diminished–and along with it much of Lucky Strike's customer base. They went to a direct sales cash-and-carry business with all operations located on East Hollis Street. As with Lafayette Beverages and Cocheco Bottling, the business stayed in the family with son Rene "Babe" Simoneau taking over upon his father's passing in 1968. The company continued to make most of their own flavorings from scratch. A plant visitor reported seeing African ginger being extracted laboratory-style for use in the firm's ginger ale production. [86]

Lucky Strike never converted away from the returnable bottle and continued to produce some fifteen regular and twelve diet flavors in 7-ounce or 29-ounce glass bottled topped with metal crown-cork caps. Of course, by the 1980s most mainline beverage companies were using plastic bottles and aluminum cans exclusively. Rene reported in a 1985 *Nashua Telegraph* article that new glass bottles were getting harder and harder to obtain, especially for the smaller 7-ounce bottles–"the perfect size for kids." He related that when he could not obtain green glass bottles for his ginger ale, he was forced to put the product up in clear glass. It didn't sell. Consumers had become fully trained to associate green bottles with either ginger ale, some type of mixer, or the lemon-lime type sodas such as Sprite, 7Up and Squirt.

Lucky Strike would sell 25,000 cases annually during the roaring post-World War II years, mostly to the small neighborhood stores. As those localized outlets disappeared over time, so did the small bottlers' customer base. The large grocery chains preferred to do business with the major brands and those brands commanded premium shelf space and offered discounts that the independents just couldn't afford to match. The large grocery chains also moved away from accepting the returnable bottles; the mainstay of many smaller independents like Lucky Strike.

By the time of the 1985 newspaper article, the Lucky Strike Ginger Ale Company had but two employees, Rene Lagasse and his wife Susan. They were the remaining "chief cook and bottle washer" of this once thriving family enterprise. On May 14, 1988, the *Boston Globe* reported that the Lucky Strike Ginger Ale closed its doors for good. Rene lamented that he had worked there starting at age eight and it was the one and only job that he ever held. He observed that when he started out, independent soda companies were doing a brisk business, maybe as many as a dozen located in Nashua alone. From that point on, only one independent Granite State bottler with a line of carbonated flavored tonics would remain.

That sole independent bottler is Conner Bottling Works of Newfields, New Hampshire whose story is profiled in Chapter 6.

Figure 20 The final location for the Lucky Strike Ginger Ale Co. at 37 E. Hollis St. in Nashua. As with so many of the former bottling plants, now repurposed for a different business.

6 FIZZ AND WATER SHARE THE WEALTH: 2000-PRESENT

For the American soft drink industry, the new century brought with it both totally new trends as well as a bit of "there is nothing new under the sun."

The home brewing of soft drinks is known to be an ancient practice with ginger ales and root beers, not only serving as early popular favorites but also long-running top sellers. As we saw in Chapter 3, Charles Hires perfected a specific blend of root beer and commercialized it for home use in the 1870s and 1880s. Originally a dry powder sold in packets, his home kits offered a more convenient liquid extract in bottles by 1893; a variation of that home kit was available well into the 1980s. While Hires was the most recognized and popular brand of root beer extract based on both quality and astute advertising, there were always competitors. As an example, Dr. Sayman's Root Beer Extract was created in 1903 with full instructions for home brewing handily printed on the bottle's paper label.

One of the advantages to home brewing a soft beverage like root beer was the modest cost of the final product, even with the customer providing their own bottles, caps and capping device (labels optional!). Hires and others commonly highlighted this cost-savings feature in their advertising. The modest cost of the do-it-yourself kits was especially attractive to large families living on limited incomes as store-bottled carbonated sodas might likely be considered an out-of-reach luxury.

Such was the case in my father's household during his formative years in a New Bedford, Massachusetts, three-decker dwelling. He recounts how his mother would bottle a batch of root beer and let it ferment in the attic–a seemingly risky venture under warm summer conditions. His oldest brother may have been the only family member to continue the home brew practice into adulthood, the other siblings finding the bottled beverages from the grocery store too convenient to pass up. My uncle would put up his batches and store them, not in the attic, but in his cellar–a wiser choice given the uncertainties of fermentation rates. Still, I distinctly recall visiting one summer and while my cousin and I were enjoying the latest episode of *Bonanza* on their Heathkit color TV (assembled by my uncle, a college biology teacher), we heard a minor explosion below us. In answer to my puzzled facial expression, my cousin calmly indicated that it was just "another" bottle of root beer that got too fizzy. Sure enough, next morning's investigation found the broken glass and sticky residue from his dad's DIY beverage-making activities.

THE WATER REVIVAL – A MIGHTY SURGE

The home production of carbonated soft drinks from scratch, or from a concentrate that required a decent level of effort, faded as a common practice by the 1970s. If anything, it was somewhat replaced by beer-making projects that had become popular through the use of take-home kits and by the widely-rising interest in craft beers and commercial microbrewing. What did pique the post-2000 public's interest was the at-home carbonation of flavored sparking water, as evidence by the successes of SodaStream Inc. and their namesake compact countertop units.

While traditional carbonated (sweetened) sodas are increasingly falling out of favor with many health-conscience consumers, one beverage sector benefiting from the trend is sparkling waters, including bottled sparking waters. The New England regional soft drink powerhouse Polar Beverages of Worcester, Massachusetts,[87] has captured a sizeable market share of this bottled water sector.

Interestingly, SodaStream® didn't just appear from thin air in the 2000s to capture this market niche, as it may have appeared to most of us. The company's origins date to 1903 and a famed United Kingdom gin distiller, W & A Gibley, Ltd. Gibley manufactured an "apparatus for aerating liquids," which was primarily sold to society's upper crust. (Picture your butler manipulating a large clunky device to make sparking water for the amusement of you and your well-heeled friends!) But times change, and the post-World War II consumerism-for-the-masses resulted in a true kitchen counter version of this carbonation unit that was introduced in 1955. The company also got a bit more marketing savvy than its 1903 version and created a popular slogan for the times, "Get busy with the fizzy."

After a variety of ownership changes, SodaStream® became part of the giant Cadbury Schweppes empire in 1985. By the 1990s consumers were tiring of the novelty of making their own drinks and the operations were purchased in 1998 by Soda-Club, an Israeli business venture. Relaunched in numerous countries, the SodaStream® trend caught on in a big way in the United States after going public here in 2010 on the NASDAQ exchange.

One marketing pitch that SodaStream® used extensively over the past decade relates to the potential environmental benefits of home carbonation.

The argument to be made centers around reducing packaging (throw-away plastic bottles) and virtually eliminating product transportation–neither the distributors nor the customers need to haul around weighty amounts of lightly-flavored water. Sales of SodaStream® declined after 2013 but rebounded by 2018 along with increasing store sales of bottled flavored water. SodaStream® became a wholly-owned component of PepsiCo in 2018, but the bulk of its sales continue to be in European markets. In 2020 the countertop devices could be found in a mere 1.5% of U.S. households, about two million units total. Although a market certainly still exists for the at-home carbonation devices, most consumers still prefer to purchase their fizzy water already flavored and bottled.[88]

* * *

A major consumer trend that has continued, if not accelerated, since 2000 has centered around wellness and dietary concerns. Obesity rates among adults and children alike have prompted a conscious de-emphasis on all sugary snacks, including carbonated sodas. One popular alternative the public turned to is water, specifically bottled waters – still, carbonated, flavored, fortified, and all options in between. As discussed in Chapter I, the bottling and sales of natural waters, specifically mineral and spring waters, was once a common commercial venture. By the early part of the 20th century, the availability of reliably safe municipal tap waters led to a major shift away from dependance on local springs and surface waters. In the 1970s a mere 350 million gallons of bottled water was sold in the United States.[89] Much of that was delivered in 5 -gallon glass jugs supplying the communal water coolers common to offices, governmental, and commercial buildings.

Then in 1977, that otherwise staid French water brand, Perrier, made a bold play to invade the North American marketplace. Perrier's marketing strategy was pretty straightforward but quite clever—target the growing status-conscience, affluent baby boomers by highlighting its French pedigree and premium price. As we now know, the strategy was successful and Perrier's U.S. sales of bubbly water skyrocketed from three million bottles in 1975 to 200 million just four years later. One of their taglines used in print advertising was "Perrier: Earth's First Soft Drink"—a bit of a clever stretch, but when have advertising copy writers been overly concerned with hard facts?[90]

Illustration 17 In the 1980s Perrier made a concerted effort to establish itself in the North American bottled water marketplace, often employing clever print advertisements (altered composite ad shown for effect).

Riding the wave of bottled water popularity, Perrier purchased the venerable Poland Spring Water in 1980, providing the company with an eighty-five percent share of the American bottled spring water market. In 1992 the Swiss food and beverage powerhouse, Nestlè purchased Perrier but continued to market both Perrier and Poland Spring waters along with other regional brands under its control.

As Americans grew increasingly concerned with its health, they looked for alternatives to the traditional carbonated sodas. In response to this trend, the major soft drink brands began to further diversify into other beverages such as ice teas, sports drinks, fruit beverages, and certainly bottled water. In 1994 Pepsi began test-marketing a filtered bottled water they named Aquafina and launched it nationally a few years later accompanied by a major marketing campaign. The Coca-Cola Company was a bit slower to enter the bottled water market but did so in early 1999 with their Desani; like Aquafina, it is essentially a filtered and purified tap water product.[91]

Many took great amusement with the sky-rocketing market for individually-bottled water. This was especially true with the general realization that many of the more popular offerings were not exotic mineral waters emanating from historic springs, but were simply refined municipal water. "You're willing to pay what for tap water you can get at home?" was a quite-common response. But the success of bottled water is a complex story, partly driven by overall health concerns, of course, and also partly by consumer taste[92] preferences. Largely overlooked or downplayed by critics is the absolute convenience factor provided by these non-returnable and relatively inexpensive bottles of H_2O. Americans cherish their purchasing choices, and these containers provide totally portable, self-contained, hydrating options for the busy individual on the go. Should you forget to bring a bottle or two acquired during your last grocery shopping venture, every gas station and convenient store along your route can supply a wide selection of brands and container sizes—not to mention the widely-available soft drink vending machines.[93]

Other than the high cost-per-ounce of these bottled refreshments, are there downsides to this beverage? Yes, of course. Most everything in life has its list of pluses and minuses, including bottled water. One of the biggest negatives is the bottle itself–for all intents and purposes a single-use plastic. The trade-off we incur for personal convenience is the difficulty in collecting and recycling plastics—a topic beyond the scope of this book but one that offers no small challenge.

Nevertheless, bottled water sales continued to climb in the 2000s, reaching eight billion gallons by 2006 and exceeding ten billion gallons by 2010. Sometime around 2017 water became the most popular non-alcoholic beverage in the United States, accounting for over 51 percent of soft beverage consumption. The sales surge was certainly aided by entire lines of products commonly referred to as the "enhanced water segment"–the energy waters, wellness waters, vitamin waters, protein waters and just plain flavored waters. None of these categories carry an FDA-recognition, but each is clearly oriented toward a market segment. Can these enhanced waters actually be considered bottled waters–or are they more accurately just categories of soft drinks? (refer to Appendix A for water definitions). As with the carbonated sodas, marketing of waters naturally plays a huge part in a product's success or failure.

> In 2020 we Americans consumed about 45 gallons of bottled water per person, almost triple our 1999 consumption.
> Source: Beverage Marketing Corp., 2020.

THE GRANITE STATE EXPERIENCE

In spite of its wealth of natural resources and abundant clean waters, New Hampshire does not generally enjoy the geographic identification that comes from a highly-branded bottled water like Poland Spring (Maine), Saratoga (New York) or Perrier (France). All beverage manufacturers and water bottlers in the Granite State are required to be licensed by the Department of Health and Human Services. The Beverage and Bottled Water Inspection and Licensing Program reviews testing results to determine compliance with both state and federal quality and safety standards. The definition of "beverage" in New Hampshire covers all non-alcoholic beverages–including all bottled, waters whether intended for table or medicinal use.

Roadside springs can be found throughout the country, and findaspring.com identifies thirty-one such untreated springs in the Granite State. Some are tested for potability and/or marked with disclaimers from the local authorities, many are not. The "Raw Water" or "Live Water" movement refers to consuming unfiltered and unsterilized spring water.

As of early 2022, only four companies were registered spring water suppliers in New Hampshire, and two of those currently appear inactive.

Monadnock Mountain Spring Water Company has been in operation since 1987 and manages a sizable bottled water distribution concern out of Wilton, New Hampshire. Monadnock bottles half-liter and gallon containers for retail shelf space in stores and member clubs. A significant portion of its business, though, involves delivery of 5-gallon water cooler bottles and packaged smaller containers to businesses, institutions, and residences throughout the southern-central part of the state using its own fleet vehicles. The company advertises its products as "New Hampshire's Own 100% Natural Spring Water." The source is an extensive glacial aquifer in Wilton on the site of the bottling plant and, as with virtually all spring water suppliers, the water is filtered through sediment and activated charcoal filters prior to ozonation and bottling.[94]

Monadnock Mountain Spring Water company operates a self-service vending station at their bottling plant in Wilton. Open 24 hours a day, 7 days a week, one can fill their own containers with delicious spring water for just $0.35 per gallon. Monadnockspring.com.

The Castle Springs Bottling Company in Moultonborough was originally associated with the 5,500-acre mountaintop Castle in the Clouds historical site and tourist attraction. The spring water operation was founded in 1970 and offered a variety of bottle sizes with attractive labels and equally attractive print advertisements. Ads played upon the popularity and natural setting of the Lake Winnipesaukee region, suggesting their brand offered some of the purest water available anywhere.

In 2003 the bottled water operations became part of the national CG Roxane enterprise. Family-owned Roxane is headquartered in California and operates seven natural springs with associated "at the source" bottling plants. In addition to New Hampshire, the company has bottling facilities in California, Arkansas, South Carolina, Tennessee and New York. Spring water products are marketed and sold under the name Crystal Geyer® Alpine Spring Water®[95].

One New Hampshire spring water firm that benefited from a recognizable name and seemingly had a promising future was the Balsams Spring Water Company. Like Castle Springs Bottling, Balsams started through an association with a famed New Hampshire location, in this case the Balsams Grand Resort of Dixville Notch in the White Mountains. The Balsams' complex of upscale hotel and summer and winter recreational facilities included an on-site spring house. There, guests could avail themselves of the high-quality spring water coming from the surrounding lofty metamorphic peaks.

In early 1985, The Balsams Spring Water Company was created to facilitate the commercialization of this water source and met with some success. Spring water was stored in tanks and trucked in bulk off-site for bottling and distribution. One specialty market pursued by the company was "Baby Water," a name they trademarked for a time with the hope that it would find success with mothers desiring to use natural spring water to prepare their baby formulas. In 1994 the entire spring water concern was sold to the well-established juice bottler, Veryfine based in northern Massachusetts. But the retail water business did not develop as all had hoped and Veryfine itself was sold to Kraft Foods in 2004, ending the Balsams spring water venture.

* * *

Four other beverage operations from the Granite State are worthy of closer examination and represent the range of business potential missed and business potential fulfilled. One of these, Twin Mountain Spring Water Company, could be a major player in todays' retail bottled water market were it not for the machinations of corporate decisions. Three other firms represent the spectrum of successful soft drink bottling concerns from three very different positions. Coca-Cola Beverages Northeast is a premier bottler of that brand's water, carbonated and non-carbonated beverages. Private Label Specialties, Ltd. offers a selection of sparkling waters and custom-flavored carbonated sodas with personalized labels for businesses, associations, institutions and individuals. Conner Bottling Works/Squamscot Beverages, operated by the same family since its founding in 1863, simply represents the iconic New Hampshire fizzy tonic experience of both yesteryear and today.

TWIN MOUNTAIN SPRING WATER COMPANY, NASHUA

One of New Hampshire's most interesting and commercially-aggressive ventures into the bottled spring water market occurred not in the Lakes Region or White Mountains but in north Nashua. To add intrigue to the backstory, this company moved into a building that had previously housed a division of a Cold War spy firm known as ITEK. Investor Laurance Rockefeller helped create this defense contractor in 1957 at the height of the Cold War. The firm's primary specialty was developing high-resolution cameras for use on CIA spy satellites. Later, because of its expertise in optical physics, the firm was asked to analyze and enhance the famous Zapruder film, the only known video evidence of the 1963 assassination of President John F. Kennedy.[96]

Alas though, the 65,000 square-foot Nashua building that the Twin Mountain Spring Water Company took possession of in 1994 formerly housed one of ITEK's least sexy business divisions. ITEK Nashua manufactured digital phototypesetting equipment for the printing industry. Boring! Still, the Cellu Drive building was perfect for Twin Mountain owner Mike Poor's vision–a modern water bottling plant to serve high-volume grocery chains and the custom bottling market.[97]

The building's size more than doubled within the first two years with the addition of expanded production and warehouse space. State of the art bottling equipment was acquired and operations were off and running. The plant bottled SunBurst Fruit Juices in HDPE (opaque high- density polyethylene) bottles, a business Poor had started in Salem, Massachusetts, in 1949.

The plant's mainstay product was of course spring water. Even though Twin Mountain was in the name of the company, spring water was not obtained from that White Mountain locale–the area was simply a favorite of Mike Poor and his wife. Spring water was procured from the Alton Bay area in New Hampshire and from Stockbridge, Vermont, just north of Killington. Tanker trucks with an 8,000-gallon capacity would off-load water into stainless steel holding tanks at the Nashua facility at the rate of one every few hours. The water was filtered and ozonated before bottling in PET (clear polyethylene terephthalate, a form of polyester). PET bottles are superior to HDPE bottles because they do not "breath" and thus they prevent odors from permeating into the product. This preserves the original characteristics of the spring water and extends its shelf life. Labeled bottles would then be packaged and distribution to grocery store shelves through the region.

Twin Mountain also served as a private-label bottler supplying branded spring water to some of the supermarket chains, such as Stop & Shop and retail restaurants like Sbarro. Interestingly, one of the company's private-label clients was Coca-Cola Bottling Company of Northern New England (CCNNE, renamed Coca-Cola Beverages Northeast after October 2019). CCNNE is an independent bottler of Coca-Cola products and in the mid-1990s wanted to offer its distribution network a spring water product to compete in that growing sector. CCNNE trademarked the name Glacial Mist[98] in 1993 and had Twin Mountain supply it with bottle spring water starting around 1996. Ironically, one of the state's largest Coke bottling plants had been located on Amherst Street in Nashua, literally a stone's throw from the Twin Mountain plant (this older plant was being phased out during this period with production shifted elsewhere). The Glacial Mist product was relatively short-lived when The Coca-Cola Company prioritized and fast-tracked the launching of the Desani water brand in early 1999, as previously noted.

Twin Mountain also developed a flavored spring water product they called The Guzzler, with flavors such as tropical punch and kiwi-strawberry.[99] This popular product line was primarily distributed to grocery chains and big-box retail stores. The management of Twin Mountain wasn't afraid to experiment with product development and for a short while in 1996 produced a caffeinated spring water they trademarked as JAVAQUA. This offering was dropped in short order, however, as the caffeine additive caused the water to turn a yellow tint during storage–definitely not a consumer-appealing effect.

Like most soft drink bottlers, Twin Mountain's workforce would typically peak during the summer months of high production and often exceed 100 workers at those times. But in 1999 the ownership was bought out by American Beverage Corporation (ABC) with the provision that the Nashua facility operate in that location for a minimum of five years. Unfortunately, ABC was perhaps not the best manager of a spring water plant. In a cost-cutting move they procured water closer to Nashua by using a spring at Dram Cup Hill in nearby Milford. But this water source proved to be inferior and carried a less than desirable taste, which drew customer complaints. The Milford source was soon dropped.

Then in 2006, citing high electricity prices in New England, ABC first moved the fruit juice line and then the remainder of the Nashua plant's equipment to Pennsylvania. This effectively brought an end to the company's spring water sales. ABC was itself sold later, but the Guzzler Fruit Drink is still produced today by Harvest Hill Beverage Company which also owns the Veryfine brand. The Cellu Drive building was sold to Worthen Industries, in 2007 who converted it to a facility to extrude films and coat substrates for the apparel, footwear, medical equipment and other industrial sectors. The plant operates in that capacity today[100].

Figure 21 The last remnants of Nashua's Twin Mountain Spring Water operation are removed in 2017. Three stainless steel tanks up to 16,000 gal capacity were used to store spring water trucked in from the Lakes Region prior to filtration and bottling.

* * *

After peaking in the late 1990s, per capita soft drink consumption fell every year after 2000, losing ground to the non-carbonated options like water and fruit-based drinks. Still, about half of all Americans drink carbonated soda every day, accounting for some $2.9 billion in annual sales for the beverage industry.

What flavors of carbonated sodas are popular in the U.S. today? A 2019 industry survey concluded that, not surprisingly, cola dominates the market. The breakdown included:[101]

Cola	50.9%
Heavy Citrus	11.3%
Lemon-line	10.7%
Pepper*	10.8%
Orange	5%
Root Beer	3.4%
All others	7.9%

*This category generally represents the Dr Pepper/Pibb spicy-cherry type offerings

COCA-COLA BEVERAGES NORTHEAST, LONDONDERRY/BEDFORD

It is probably not overly surprising that Coca-Cola, the crown-king of cola beverages, made its mark on the Northeast, including the Granite State. But with its southern origin and early distribution system that concentrated on the Southeast and Midwest, Coca-Cola was a relatively slow-starter in the Northeast. By 1909 Coke was bottled at almost 400 locations, but most of these were small, family-owned bottlers within a couple of states' drive from Atlanta. By 1915 Florida alone counted forty-seven Coke bottlers, Kentucky nine and even large Northeast states like New Jersey and New York could only boast one and two locations respectively. New Englanders were still quite fond of their Lowell-based Moxie and the myriad of root beer and ginger ale choices that appealed to the Yankee palate. In 1920 Moxie still outsold Coca-Cola, a telling fact when considering today's taste preferences and associated beverage sales.

Seeing the promise of the cola drink that was so popular south and west of New England, two enterprising brothers, Clemens O. and Charles A. Seifert, purchased the Haverhill, Massachusetts Coca-Cola operations in 1919. Two years later they moved the plant to 23 South Broadway in Salem Depot, New Hampshire, establishing the state's first Coke plant with the goal of making true believers out of Granite Staters. They were pioneers of sorts, and the state's second Coca-Cola bottling facility didn't arrive until 1944 (in Manchester). Other plants followed in the subsequent decades as the state's population, and thirst, grew.

Figure 22 The delivery fleet of New Hampshire's first Coca-Cola bottling enterprise, Salem, ca. 1924. Credit: Manchester Historic Association.

The seeds for what would be the largest consolidated Coca-Cola bottler in New Hampshire were spouted in 1977 in Laconia. The Japanese holding company, Kirin Holdings, was involved with beer brewing and wanted to expand into soft beverages. They, along with businessman Roger D. Williams (a former Coca-Cola executive and descendant of the founder of Rhode Island), purchased Lakes Region Coca-Cola's operations and named the new venture KW, Inc. (Kirin and Williams) headquartered in Bedford.[102]

KW would go on to acquire Lowell (MA) Coca-Cola, which included a Fitchburg branch in 1978 and then locations in Middletown, CT, and the New Hampshire operations in Salem, Plaistow, and Manchester followed. In 1988 KW, Inc. purchased Coca-Cola of Northern New England, Inc. (CCNNE) and adopted its business name. CCNNE's plan was to consolidate and modernize its New Hampshire operations to stay abreast of the growing demand from in-state consumers as well as those in adjacent territories. In 1989 the firm constructed a new 150,000 square foot production center on a 78-acre industrial parcel in Londonderry. Expansion over the following years pushed the plant's size to almost 500,000 square feet.

Figure 23 Cranking out the product. Empty cans are stacked ready for filling at Coke Northeast's Londonderry production facility.

Figure 24 Coca-Cola Beverages Northeast in Londonderry represents a thoroughly modern and efficient soft drink bottling plant in today's marketplace.

In 2007 CCNNE branched out from its primary efforts of bottling and distributing to acquire the Moxie brand from Monarch NuGrape of Atlanta. CCNNE's Londonderry facility had been bottling Moxie under contract for some time but brought the storied brand in-house under its affiliate, Cornucopia Beverages. Headquartered in Bedford and renamed the Moxie Beverage Company, the iconic beverage was relaunched with a new tagline, Live Your Life With Moxie! Marketing initiatives included a bright orange trailer truck with the distinctive Moxie Boy image gracing its side panels. The Moxie Beverage Company also generously supported such events as the annual Moxie Festival held in Lisbon Falls, Maine, and the Pease Greeters, a group of volunteers who met flights of U.S. service personnel returning from combat areas through the Pease International Tradeport in Portsmouth. Well over 10,000 cans of Moxie were provided to these returning heroes until the COVID-19 pandemic forced a halt to the program.[103]

In October 2017 CCNNE closed a deal to acquire sales territory from The Coca-Cola Company (TCCC) across eight states in the Northeast as part of the Atlanta company's plan to divest its bottling operations and refranchise its North American operations. This was a huge leap forward for CCNNE with the addition of two more bottling centers and a wide distribution territory. By 2022 the organization had grown to 3,400 employees (700 in NH) overseeing an expanded portfolio of products from the namesake Coke line to Canada Dry, Fanta and Dr Pepper sodas, Desani waters, smartwater, vitaminwater, and a selection of energy drinks, ice teas and coffees. Londonderry/Bedford remains the primary control center–the mothership of this expanded enterprise. In 2019 the organization's name changed to Coca-Cola Beverages Northeast (Coke Northeast) to reflect the wider market it now serves.[104]

There was one change that came about during this period of Coke Northeast's territorial expansion that concerned Moxie fans–that brand, held for some eleven years was sold to TCCC in December 2018.[105] The sale of the Moxie brand ownership no doubt permitted Coke Northeast to better focus on making and distributing its product lines and not get distracted with managing a specialty brand like Moxie. As one would expect, Moxie soda sales at approximately 175,000 cases a year represent just a small fraction of Coke Northeast's annual production output from the Londonderry production center of thirty-two million cases. Moxie loyalists however were greatly concerned that TCCC might simply ignore their favorite brand and possibly even cease production of this fizzy beverage that has been bottled continuously since March 1885. So far, those fears seem unfounded, as Coke

Northeast's modern Londonderry center continues to produce Moxie and Diet Moxie in cans and plastic bottles for distribution to the faithful. Except for the glass-bottled, cane sugar Moxie from either Orca Beverage, Inc. in the Pacific Northwest, or Pennsylvania's Catawissa Bottling Company, all commercially-available Moxie comes courtesy of the dedicated Coke Northeast soda elves working diligently in the Londonderry production facility.

* * *

PRIVATE LABEL SPECIALTIES, LTD., GOFFSTOWN

Founder Ray Duhaime started out in 1991 with a simple idea–private label sparking water to offer customers something the big brands like Perrier couldn't. And what exactly was that? The opportunity for businesses and other organizations to brand their own products – to offer their customers or members something personalized, something special. Duhaime quickly found his idea resonated well with a wide array of clients in New Hampshire and beyond–restaurants, corner pizza parlors, workout gyms, new car dealerships, banks, organizations holding anniversary or commemorative events, and anyone desiring a clever way to project their brand to THEIR customers.[106]

From the initial offering of sparking water, customers asked for more options and Duhaime worked with flavoring chemists to develop an old-fashioned style root beer soda, which remains the most popular flavor among his clients. The expanded current suite of fourteen flavored offerings includes such standbys as black cherry, orange cream, strawberry and golden ginger ale, all offered in 12-ounce glass bottles. Further reflecting the company's responsiveness to customer suggestion, Private Label Specialties has just added a brightly colored lemon-lime flavor to their carbonated soda lineup.

The carbonated offerings are produced at the company's modern bottling facility in Goffstown using formulations developed specifically for them by the flavor laboratories they employ. The spring water products are bottled are at their source with most of the water coming from a protected, low-hardness spring in the hilly wooded terrain of northern Pennsylvania's Poconos. As with the rest of the beverage industry, the company finds that consumer demand for bottled beverages tends to peak in the warm summer months.

Since Private Label Specialties serves clientele in all fifty states and anywhere that package delivery services offer, including a recently fulfilled an order from Australia, what sets them apart from others? Aside from offering high-quality products, Ray Duhaime believes it is their uniquely New Hampshire-styled flexibility and versatility. His company cheerfully works with customers from those desiring a single case of custom-labeled beverages to those requiring ten trailer truck loads. Most other custom-label beverage providers are primarily oriented toward the high-volume sales and not eager to serve the smaller buyers who are also trying hard to promote their establishments' brand recognition.

And what might be founder Ray Duhaime's favorite soda flavor? Without hesitation, he cannot resist his own root beer formulation–his clients' perennial favorite and the "flagship" of the company.

Figure 25 An example of the custom-labeled sodas provided by Private Label Specialties of Bedford. New Boston has seen a long lineage of Dodges as merchants starting with Charles W. Dodge in 1868.

* * *

CONNER BOTTLING WORKS/SQUAMSCOT BEVERAGES, NEWFIELDS

Figure 26 Conner Beverages' wooden crate displayed in front of their Newfields bottling works.

And then there was one. The last independent, fully-retail bottler of carbonated sodas in New Hampshire is Conner Bottling Works of Newfields, with their Squamscot Old Fashioned Beverage line. This family-owned, family-run, 160-year-old business is nothing short of a Granite State institution in today's otherwise automated, digitized, monetized era.

In 1863 on the 40-acre family farm in rural Newfields less than half a mile from the tidal Squamscott River, William H. Conner started his business by bottling beer for others. The kegged product was shipped to Newfields via rail line from one or more of three Portsmouth brew houses of the time.

Somewhere in this timeframe Conner also started producing a line of flavored tonics he branded as Connermade. Non-alcoholic spruce beer and ginger ale were put up in glass bottles using the same style porcelain stoppers and a wire bail closure employed for the beer. Paper labels on the embossed, clear-glass bottles readied the product for sale and distribution to the public. William Conner ran the business until his passing in 1911 when his son Alfred Sr. took the reins. At that point the family venture was producing a modest 4,115 cases of soft beverages annually.[107]

Modest growth continued until the years of National Prohibition, when the business experienced a decided uptick, especially of its popular ginger ale soda. By 1930, when the family was offering fourteen flavor choices and selling nearly 26,000 cases a year, it was decided to change the brand name to Squamscot Beverages. Reportedly the name was chosen to reflect the area's Native American history and culture. The Msquamskek or M'Squamskook (translated as "falls at the place of the salmon") were among the first to inhabit the coastal shores of the Great Bay estuary and the banks of the Squamscott River in what are now the towns of Exeter, Newfields and Stratham.

The modern bottling era came to the Conners' operation in 1938 when Alfred Sr. bought a brand-new Crown Cork & Seal Dixie Model F single head syruper-filler. Fed by a 60-gallon glass-lined tank in the syrup room above, the Dixie combines a dose of flavored syrup with chilled carbonated water in glass bottles and seals the deal with a cork-lined metal crown cap (invented by Crown Cork & Seal founder William Painter in 1892). On a good day when the Dixie is behaving, the modest operation can bottle over 30 cases worth of fizzy beverage each hour.

Figure 27 Squamscot vintage quart bottle reflecting the area's Native American roots.

When Alfred Sr. passed away in 1948, it was his son Alfred Jr. who took over the family beverage business, and eventually Jr.'s son Tom and then grandson Dan joined in turn. Alfred Jr. retired in the mid 1990s, but as his son Tom likes to lightheartedly relate, "He never missed a day of work after that!" Alfred Jr. remained involved in the family business at various levels until passing away at age ninety-four in 2008.

Like most every other independent bottler, by the 1970s and 80s the Conners found it increasingly difficult to compete against the national brands who were able to command the majority of shelf space at the large grocery chains. To diversify their business activities, they also began to distribute products for others and represented brands such as White Rock beverages (originally founded by a Wisconsin pharmacist but now headquartered in New York City) and Very Fine products (founded in Massachusetts).

As with Lucky Strike Ginger Ale, the returnable bottle issue also became a major dilemma for the Conner Bottling Works. It became increasingly difficult to find glass manufacturers for the heavy returnable bottles and eventually they came to rely on a supplier based in Trinidad. But the major stumbling block turned out to be us–the consumers. Collectively, we grew weary of carting bags and cartons of heavy empty bottles back to the stores and concluded that the deposit fee just wasn't enticing enough for us to bother with that chore. Bottlers could no longer count on getting their bottles back to clean, refill, and send back out brimming with their bubbly, tasty product.

In 1997 the Conners switched to using clear, non-returnable glass bottles–in large part to save their traditional Squamscot Beverage line altogether and continue to pay tribute to their family's long heritage. With this switch the quart size beverage bottles were discontinued to concentrate on producing the single serving size that continues to this day. And of course, the bottles with their painted/baked-on Applied Colored Labels (ACL) became history as well–replaced with modern paper labels. The most recent shipment of bottles came to Newfields from a glass producer in Panama. The retired Squamscot ACL bottles are now highly prized by collectors.

The 1938-era Dixie is still on the job today, serving as the company's sole bottler and sitting exactly where it was placed when originally delivered–no retirement in sight. However, keeping "her" running reliably is a constant challenge, and long-time operator Tom Howcroft is careful not to "rile her" by saying anything too critical while within earshot. New parts are non-existent, so the Conners have resorted to buying other Dixie units as they become available to salvage critical parts, or in some cases they are forced to manufacture replacement components. Tom Conner has confessed to having a possible back-up plan–a 1962 bottling system in storage on the property which was acquired from a former Coca-Cola plant where it was used for a mere eighteen months.

Figure 28 Squamscot's Tom Howcroft at the venerable Dixie bottler working on a batch of Cherry Cola tonic.

The Squamscot Beverage line currently consists of twenty-seven flavors. The Conners like to point out that their customers very much appreciate this wide array of choices, even if many of them are prone to ordering the half-dozen most popular flavors over and over. However, if a customer orders a full shipment of say, just strawberry flavor, then the Conners will happily oblige and run strawberry on the Dixie until the order is filled. Sometimes large orders can be challenging due to the small workforce and the limitations of the Dixie system. Conner Bottling Works tends to use the winter and spring months to build inventory in anticipation of the high-demand summer season. In times past they could accommodate a California retailer who would order two railroad cars worth of Squamscot product annually. But these days the bottling operations concentrate on keeping the local and New England regional customers fully supplied and happy. A continuous flurry of year-around bottling and distribution activities is required to fulfill just their regular orders.

The most popular of the twenty-seven flavors offered by Conner Bottling Works? Ginger Beer followed closely by Squamscot Root Beer remain the most popular. Ironically, ginger beer is among the most expensive flavors to formulate due to its ingredients; however, it is a strong seller at the New Hampshire state liquor stores due to its popularity as a mixer. For the same reason Tonic Water pulls in at third place, followed by Maple Cream and then a close tie between Cream Soda, Orange and Lemon-Lime.

Figure 29 A selection of the many Squamscot Beverage flavors available today.

What about failed flavors? The Conner family will admit to once attempting to create a New Hampshire "gift basket" using apple, blueberry and maple cream sodas. The apple wasn't especially popular and a superior-tasting blueberry turned out to be overly expensive to produce. Only the maple cream flavor survived that particular marketing venture. And while Mistletoe Mist is quite popular around the Christmas season, other holiday flavor attempts like Candy Cane and Gingerbread did not fare well.

In 2023 the Conner Bottling Works celebrates 160 years of continual operation at its original location. Believe it or not, that feat may well peg Conner as not just New Hampshire's oldest such enterprise, but the world's oldest as well. Yes, the pioneering European Schweppes was bottling soda waters in the late 1700s and created an "aerated lemonade" in 1835. But the company did not maintain any one manufacturing site continually through those years, and its soft drink production ceased entirely during World War II. So, the relatively humble operations of Conner Bottling in little Newfields,

New Hampshire, may in fact rightly hold the title of "world's oldest continuous soda bottler."

Figure 30 Author's grandson enjoying an old fashion refreshment while engaged in modern media.

What is certain beyond doubt, as the remaining flagship for the Granite State's long and illustrious independent soft drink bottling industry, the family has crafted a balanced path between tradition and innovation. How many other 160-year-old independent bottlers can also claim to generate 100 percent of their required electricity through an on-site solar voltaic array? In New Hampshire, Squamscot Old Fashion Beverages stand apart and remain on course to provide a high-quality fizzy refreshment for many more years to come.

CONCLUSION

From the mid-1800s through today, New Hampshire has hosted at least 205 carbonated soda and spring water bottlers based from some sixty Granite State cities and towns. As we've seen, the vast majority of these were small, local operations. Some consisted of a single proprietor with perhaps a helper or two, many times a family member. Sadly, most survived as viable businesses for only a very brief period before fading from the scene. They are now remembered by single-line notations in vintage city directories, yellowed newspaper advertisements, or dusty embossed bottles gracing the shelves of our State's antique shops and flea markets.

There was, however, a smaller, but not insignificant, group of "tonic" bottlers that did find a decent measure of success and enjoyed much longer periods of serving the New Hampshire citizenry before succumbing to business hurdles or difficult economic times. Many of these entities started as small, independent bottlers of their own formulations but transitioned to contract bottlers for the "big guys" such as Coca-Cola, PepsiCo, Hires, or Canada Dry. Others merged or partnered with fellow businesses—even competitors—often surrendering their unique identity. In this manner they survived and maybe even thrived for a number of years, until the continuing industry consolidation and economies of scale were too much for them to overcome.

Some of those more notable Granite State bottlers are presented in the following table. It is important to realize that each of these listed enterprises may have used a number of variations of the names listed here and that the years of operation represent a digestion of best-available information from city directories, beverage industry directories, local history records, or just surviving embossed and labeled soda bottles.

Conclusion Table 1. Former New Hampshire Carbonated Soft Drink Bottlers That Demonstrated Considerable Staying Power.

Those listed below were known to have bottle carbonated flavored sodas, but in a number of cases either spring water or beer may have often constituted the majority of their bottled production. Companies changed their product lines over the years, and precise production records for these now-defunct independent bottlers are virtually nonexistent.

Town/City	Company Name(s)	Operational	Total Yrs
Atkinson Depot	Granite State Spring Water Co./Hi-Brow Beverages	1896-1928	32
Claremont	Claremont Soda Works/Hies/PepsiCo	1920-1955	35+
Claremont	Bob Schneider Inc.	1946-1970	24
Concord	Aetna Bottling Co.	1885-1924	39
Concord	Granite Bottling Co.	1885-1929	44
Concord	Rumford Bottling Works/Spur Bottling Co.	1904-1955	51
Concord	Whistle Bottling Works/Coca-Cola Bottling Co.	1920-1950	30
Derry/Manchester	Lafayette Bottling Co./Derry Mineral Spring Water	1882-1986	104

Conclusion

Town/City	Company Name(s)	Operational	Total Yrs
Dover	Cassidy & Co./Dover Bottling Co.	1922-1942	20
Dover	Robinson Bros./Garrison Hill Beverages	1898-1960	62
Keene	N.G. Gurnsey & Sons	1885-1972	87+
Laconia	Lawrence Baldi Co.	1920-1948	26
Manchester	Cott Bottling Co./Silver Brothers	1948-1972	24
Manchester	Derby Club Beverage Co.	1934-1955	21
Manchester	Green Mountain Ginger Ale Co.	1927-1950	23
Manchester	Manchester Tonic Co./Kleer-Kool Beverages	1924-1950	26
Manchester	Queen City Bottling Co.	1920-1950	30
Manchester	Rock Spring/Bo-La	1906-1965	59
Manchester	Robert Schneider/Gustave Schneider/Hires Bottling	1885-1950	65
Milford	Milford Bottling Co.	1920-1960	40
Nashua	J.J. McGlynn Bottling Works	1916-1950	34
Nashua/Hudson	Nashua Bottling Co.	1918-1954	37
Nashua	Lucky Strike Ginger Ale Co./ Simoneau Bottling Co.	1922-1988	66
Newport	Newport Bottling Co./ Budd's Best Beverages	1916-1972	56
North Conway	White Mountain Beverage Co.	1922-1950	38
North Conway	Varsity Beverage Co./PepsiCo	1947-1988	41
Plaistow	C. Leary & Co.	1946-1970	24
Portsmouth	Boynton Bottling Works/Coca-Cola	1873-1950	77
Portsmouth	Hartford & Raitt Bottling Co.	1911-1955	44
Portsmouth	Laughlin Bottling Works/PepsiCo/Canada Dry	1887-1972	85
Rochester	Cocheco Bottling Works/Emerson & Company	1890-1977	87
Somersworth	W.A. Horne Bottling Co./Spur Bottling Co.	1901-1949	48
Somersworth	St. Hilaire Bottling Works/Coca-Cola Bottling	1910-1988	78

Town/City	Company Name(s)	Operational	Total Yrs
Stark	Stark Spring Water Co.	1935-1955	23

As we saw in Chapter 6, the reigning two "crown princes" (pun intended) of today's New Hampshire carbonated soft drink scene:

Londonderry/Bedford's Coca-Coca Beverages Northeast–with roots back to the Salem Coke operation of 1921, and

Newfields' Conner Bottling Works/Squamscot Beverages–with roots back to 1863 and remaining under family ownership and operation at its original location.

Somewhat ironically, within our relatively small state we have one of the most modern and efficient commercial bottling operations in the soft drink industry today, AND we host the oldest continuously-operating bottling works in the entire country (and perhaps world). Together, these two enterprises represent a notable bridge between our past and present in the world of fizzy beverages.

Only two New Hampshire spring water firms that source their water in-state remain in commercial operation today. (State business licensing records list four, but two of these appear to be inactive as of early 2023.) The two sources in full commercial operation:

Monadnock Mountain Spring Water Company of Wilton–thirty-six years of operation at the same spring site, and

CG Roxane LLC /Castle Springs Bottling Company of Moultonborough–fifty-three years of operation at the same spring site.

Both of the on-going enterprises consist of thoroughly modern bottling and distribution operations, bearing no resemblance to the mystical, medical, healing-oriented practitioners of the historic past. Similar to the state's soda bottlers, many other springs were in operation for only a brief period before fading from the scene as commercial ventures. However, several New Hampshire spring water operations did exhibit significant staying power, most notably:

> Henniker Spring Water Company of Henniker–forty-nine years of operation,

> White Mountain Mineral Springs Water Company of North Conway/Redstone–forty-seven years of operation, and

> Londonderry Lithia Spring Water Company of Londonderry (bottled in Nashua)–forty-one years of operation.

The bottled water marketplace has changed considerably over the last 150 years. Today, with robust interstate commerce and global supply chains, the Granite Stater can visit their local supermarket shelves and choose from waters originating from far beyond our border. Have a taste for Hawaiian volcanic water? California Route 66 spring water? Fiji island water? Icelandic glacial water? These and many more choices are all available to the thirsty public. One might conclude that they represent almost an embarrassment of riches when safe, clean drinking water is still a rare commodity in many parts of the global community and even in some drought-stressed areas of the United States.

The final chapters for both fizzy flavored soft drinks and for bottled waters (of all types) have yet to be written. Will the current trends in consumer taste preferences continue into the next decade and beyond, or will they radically change direction? What role in that future script will be played by concerns over health and wellness (sugar, sugar substitutes), plastic containers (recycling, microplastics), and water as a threatened resource (distribution, allocations and groundwater protection)?

New Hampshire's spring waters and flavored tonics have had a unique and exciting story to tell. Some of that story has paralleled the national trends, and some of it has taken its own course in keeping with our well-established independent vein. Clearly, the full Granite State beverage story is still unfolding and its conclusion has yet to be written. We are all playing a collective role in that outcome.

APPENDIX A. DEFINITIONS FOR THE TYPES OF CONSUMABLE WATERS

In modern times the U.S. Food and Drug Administration (FDA) regulates commercially bottled water products for the safety and health of the American public. Logically, the FDA classifies water by its origin or source:

Artesian well water—This water is collected from a well that taps an aquifer—layers of porous rock, sand, and earth that contain water—which is under pressure from surrounding upper layers of rock or clay. When tapped, the pressure in the aquifer, commonly called artesian pressure, pushes the water to the surface.

Mineral water—This water comes from an underground source and contains at least 250 parts per million total dissolved solids (TDS) in a fairly constant concentration and proportion. Minerals and trace elements must come from the geologic source of the underground water - they cannot be added during processing.

Spring water—Derived from an underground formation from which water flows naturally to the surface, this water must be collected only at the spring or through a well that taps the underground formation feeding the spring. If extracting the water through a well, the water must have the same composition and quality as the water that flowed naturally to the land surface.

Well water—This is water from a hole bored or drilled well into the ground, which taps into a bedrock or surficial aquifer that can be extracted (pumped).

Municipal water—In common terms, we're talking tap water here. The water's origin may be from a surface reservoir or groundwater extraction wells, or a blend. As delivered, it is typically treated to remove sediment, color, or other materials. It is most often chlorinated, and possibly fluoridated, before it is delivered to the point of use for the consumer.

Water from any of the above sources may be commercially bottled for public consumption. The FDA regulations have additional stipulations concerning the required production conditions during the handling, storage and bottling processes, and ultimately the standard of quality (chemical, physical and microbiological) for the finished water offered to the public.

But we're not quite done with terms and definitions for this humble substance – water. Bottled consumer beverages that are labeled as *sparking water, seltzer water, soda water, club soda* or *tonic water* are NOT considered waters by the FDA, but rather are classified as soft drinks.

Sparkling water—often a general term for any type of water that is carbonated.

Seltzer—any carbonated water without anything further additives.

Soda water or club soda—carbonated water with minerals added (commonly sodium).

Tonic water—carbonated water with quinine added for flavor.

Still water—uncarbonated water (not typically bottled but served directly in eating establishments, on airlines, etc.). In most cases the origin is local tap water.

31 A selection of New Hampshire soda bottles from the many brands and styles in use over the years.

ENDNOTES

[1] Excerpt from *I Remember Cape Cod* by E.C. Janes, copyright © 1974 by E.C. Janes. Used by permission of Viking Books, an imprint of Penguin Publishing Group, a division of Penguin Random House LLC. All rights reserved.

[2] The Saratoga Springs information presented in this chapter was compiled from numerous historical sources with the primary source: *A History of the American Soft Drink Industry, 1807-1957*, John J. Riley, 1972.

[3] In fact, this often-cited reference to a Jackson's Spa cannot be fully substantiated. Published references can be traced back to the well-respected 1970 Cecil Munsey's *Illustrated Guide to Collecting Bottles*. But unfortunately, Munsey provides no citation for his source, and researchers at the Massachusetts Historical Association can find no independent record of a Jackson's Spa in Boston or the surrounding areas. Thus, it may be simply folklore.

[4] Interestingly, parts of New England, especially in eastern and central Massachusetts, adopted the *spa* term for local grocery or convenience stores, especially those that offered soda fountain service (with "bubbly" water of course). The local soda fountain, as part of either a corner variety, pharmacy or 5 & 10 Cents store, has been an institution in America for a very long time (see Chapter 3). More than a few such examples of variety stores that are still called *spas* can be found today in some Boston and Worcester, Massachusetts neighborhoods.

[5] The Gorham community disbanded in 1819 and sold their land to the Town of Gorham. Poland Hill was a community for ten short years, disbanding in 1793. The Alfred community lasted until 1931. Sabbathday Lake officially ceased accepting new members when Elder Delmer Wilson passed away in 1961.

[6] The Poland Springs information presented in this chapter was compiled from numerous historical sources but a primary source was *Poland Spring, A Tale of a Gilded Age 1860-1900*, David L. Richards, 2005.

[7] *Mineral Resources of the United States*. U.S. Bureau of Miners Report, 1909.

[8] "Quality of Water in the Fractured Bedrock Aquifer of New Hampshire." *USGS Scientific Investigations Report 2002-5093*, Richard B. Moore, 2004.

[9] Locally pronounced "po-NĒ-mă." While there is a Ponemah Road and a well-known Ponemah Bog natural area in the town of Amherst, no one is certain of the name's origin. Ponemah towns in Illinois and Minnesota reportedly were named for an Ojbway word for "later" or "afterwards," or possibly "everlasting," and the place name appears in Henry Wadsworth Longfellow's *Song of Hiawatha*. The origin of Amherst's Ponemah remains a bit of a mystery.

[10] *Ponemah and the Milford Mineral Springs, Illustrated*. Mineral Springs Co., 1884, 25 pp.

[11] "Hotel Ponemah Destroyed by Fire." *The Milford Cabinet and Wilton Journals*. June 2, 1921.

[12] The primary sources for information on Cohas Springs came from Steve Young of ImageAbility (cohas.parmenterfarm.org) and from email correspondence with author/researcher Ed Brouder in February 2021. Brouder shared copies of historic newspaper articles and excerpts from his 2006 book with Maurice Quirin, *Manchester Airport: Flying Through Time*. Young shared a wealth of digitized photographs and illustrations, some of which were reproduced for this chapter.

[13] *Facts About Cohas Spring Water*. Cohasaukee Corporation, Manchester, NH. Accessed at the research files of the Manchester (NH) Historic Association, catalog No. 2016.073.001.

[14] "Public Invited to Inspect New Plant." *The Manchester Leader and Evening Union*, June 12, 1922, p12. This same newspaper article reported the consolidation of Brobeco with three well-known Manchester bottlers: William Glancy, Joseph Quirin, and Adolph Wagner to form a stock company with the intent of distributing "all kinds of soft drinks, ice cream, cakes and other dainty lunch products." A new plant was

planned for Second Street in Manchester and reportedly combined operations would result in the largest establishment of its type in New Hampshire. The Second Street plant and the company's lofty goals never became a reality.

[15] A primary source for much of the information on this spring was Steve Young of ImageAbility (Londonderrylithia.com and email correspondence). Young also provided accessed to his files of digitized illustrations and photographs. Another key source was Richard Holmes "Londonderry's Brief Bottled Water Fame." Derry News, September 2, 2016.

[16] As modern consumers we largely face the same challenge in sorting fact from fiction. Is that five-star product review posted on the internet from an actual purchaser/user? Or was it the fanciful work of a paid advertising company wag?

[17] "Misbranded Drugs & Foods, Londonderry Lithia Water." *Journal of the American Medical Association*, 1912, p.55.

[18] Halvorson's 1882 chemical analysis of the Londonderry spring water equated to a lithium concentration greater than 15 parts per million (ppm), which would represent a considerable concentration for natural waters anywhere in the United States. A recent study by the USGS of lithium in groundwaters from 3,140 wells used for drinking water reported a median concentration of 0.0081 ppm with no wells in New England exceeding 0.005 ppm.

[19] "Temple Mineral Spring Not Necessarily Natural." Nashua Telegraph, May 24, 2015.

[20] "Botanic Remedies in Colonial Massachusetts, 1620-1820." George E. Gifford, Jr., 1980.

[21] Avid antique and historic bottle collectors have long claimed there were as many as 110,000 proprietary liquid medicines on the market in 1900.

[22] *Elixirs, Nerve Tonics and Panaceas: The Medicine Trade in Nineteenth-Century New Hampshire.* Christopher R. DeCorse, 1984.

[23] When Ring brought Peterborough chemist Elisha Tubbs the hair restorer he had been peddling, Tubbs declared it a "dangerous fake" but offered his own formula instead. Their partner was Person Cheney, who would go on to serve as Governor (1875-1877) and then in the U.S. Senate. Ring bought out both partners after a few years.

[24] An emphasis on good health seems to have been important to Shaker communities with attention given to diet, sanitation, workplace conditions (ventilation, lighting, etc.) as well as a general focus on "cleanliness."

[25] *The Shakers And Their Proprietary Medicines*, J. Worth Estes, 1991.

[26] Estes. 1991.

[27] *Shaker House-Keeping*, Mary Whitcher. 1882

[28] The greatest number of new arrivals (converts) to the Canterbury Village Community occurred in the decade of the 1880s, with declines each decade thereafter.

[29] *Canterbury Shaker Village: Medicines As Seen Through Archeological Artifacts*, Elizabeth B. Hall, 2007.

[30] Some alcohol could be expected in almost any product derived from extracts of roots or herbs as they were typically seeped or percolated in 40-50% strength alcohol as part of the extraction process (creating a "tincture"). Alcohol was, and is, widely used because it extracts a wide range of phytochemicals and is an excellent preservative. Vanilla extract for everyday cooking is prepared in this fashion. For a vanilla extract to be labeled "pure" on the U.S., The Food and Drug Administration dictates that it must contain a minimum of 35% alcohol.

[31] *Manchester City Directories*. Accessed in the Manchester Historic Associations research library October 5, 2019.

[32] *Thall's Home Remedies*. Accessed in the Manchester Historic Associations research library August 11, 2021.

[33] *Drowning in Health: Murky of Mineral Water and Alcohol in Eighteenth-Century Medical Literature and Social Mores*, Vaugh Scribner, 2021.

[34] *Saratoga Springs: It's Mineral Waters*, S.R. Stoddard, 1806.

[35] Scribner, 2021.

[36] "Bottled Water, Spas, and Early Years of Water Chemistry." *Gound Water*, Back, Landa and Meeks, 1995.

[37] Information related to the soft drink industry throughout this chapter was compiled from numerous sources but two primary sources were: *A History of the American Soft Drink Industry, 1807-1957*, by John J. Riley, 1972, and *Organization in the Soft Drink Industry: A History of the American Bottlers of Carbonated Beverages*, by John J. Riley, 1946.

Index

[38] Tilden & Company advertising. Accessed in the on-line digital collections of the New York Public Library, digitalcollections.nypl.org, 2/15/2021.

[39] An homage to Dows' contribution to the world can be experienced first-hand at Dows Soda Fountain, an operating establishment among the many shops in the restored historic Mill No.5 complex in downtown Lowell, Massachusetts.

[40] *Dows, Gustavus D. (1828-1886).* New Hampshire Historical Society. Profile accessed at nhhistory.org, 2/15/2021.

[41] "The Soda Fountain." *American Heritage Magazine.* August 1962, Vol. 13, No.4.

[42] Riley, 1972.

[43] *Soda Popery: The History of Soft Drinks in America*, Stephen A. Tchudi, 1986.

[44] Deep-sea submersible vehicles, such as the U.S. Navy's 1960's *Trieste* bathyscaphe and the Woods Hole Oceanographic Institution's *Alvin*, have perfectly spherical passenger compartments, allowing them to withstand great depths and safely return to the surface.

[45] *Carbonated Beverages: The Art of Making, Dispensing, & Bottling Soda-Water, Mineral Waters, Ginger-Ale & Sparkling Liquors*, Thomas Chester, 1882.

[46] "The First American Soda Fountains." *Bottles and Extras.* Donald Yates, 2006.

[47] *The Manufacture of Carbonated Beverages*, Henry E. Medbery, 1945.

[48] Chester, 1882.

[49] There is no one single recipe for root beer, and there never was. Almost all recipes contain some variation of the ingredients listed in the text, as well as possibly pipsiwewa, wild cherry bark, dandelion, anise, yellow dock and a host of other possibilities. That is part of the mystique and broad appeal of root beers.

[50] All brewed "small beers," including brewed root beers will contain a trace of alcohol from the fermentation process. Typically, the alcoholic content will be one half percent or less.

[51] "Charles E. Hires Company, 1870 – Present, Philadelphia, Pennsylvania." Don Yates, *Bottles and Extras*, Summer 2005, pp.50-57.

[52] I have personally reviewed Journal No. 1, the accounting ledgers of the Moxie Nerve Food Company archived at the Matthews Museum in Union, Maine. The first two ledger entries on page one are dated March 7, 1885 for the sale of 7 pint bottles and 6 pint bottles at $.25 a bottle to two establishments in Lowell. At some point in the early 20th century Moxie would add to the date confusion by inexplicitly stating

"Since 1884" in its advertising, a practice that continues today. Such is the sometimes-strange lore of these venerable soda brands that founded a new consumer product sector over 130 years ago.

[53] *Moxie.* Arcadia Publishing. Dennis Sasseville and Merrill Lewis, 2019.

[54] Much of the information for the Dr Pepper profile was taken from the Dr Pepper Museum. Accessed at History (drpeppermuseum.com), 2021. Another invaluable source is *The Road To Dr Pepper, Texas – The Story of Dublin Dr Pepper.* Karen Wright, 2006.

[55] "How the South Cornered the Soda Market." Robert Moss, August 19, 2018, accessed at: seriouseasts.com, 2021. Entire books have been written just on the history and developments of Coca-Cola. The reader is directed to the Select Bibliography for suggestions of accomplished works on this subject.

[56] The temperance argument was widely employed in the promotion of all types of soft drinks. In the early 1900s the historic country store in Sunapee Harbor, NH (now the Anchorage Restaurant) sported a single large sign above its doorway which proclaimed, "Ice Cold Temperance Drinks" to the sober-minded villagers and tourists alike.

[57] Information related to the soft drink industry throughout this chapter was compiled from numerous sources but two primary sources were: *A History of the American Soft Drink Industry, 1807-1957,* by John J. Riley, 1972, and *Organization in the Soft Drink Industry: A History of the American Bottlers of Carbonated Beverages,* by John J. Riley, 1946.

[58] This nickname for the bottle's shape was not the official description but assigned at some point by the public. Hobbleskirts were a specific women's fashion design of the 1910s. The finished bottle contained a hefty 14.5 ounces of glass colored with a specified "German Green," later renamed "Georgia Green" after the bottler's headquarter city, Atlanta. The first contracts also specified that each bottling plant's city location would also be embossed on the bottle's bottom, thus entertaining decades of thirsty consumers and memorabilia collectors.

[59] *Vending Machines: An American Social History,* Kerry Segrave, 2002.

[60] *Soft Drink Bottlers of the United States, Volume 1, Vermont & New Hampshire,* Dennis G, Fewless and Christopher A. Weide, 2014.

[61] Fewless and Weide, 2014 (compiled from their listings).

[62] Fewless and Weide, 2014, p.212.

[63] *Fizz: How Soda Shook Up the World*, Tristan Donovan, 2014.

[64] "Business & Industry." *Upper Ashuelot, A History of Keene, New Hampshire*, A. Harold Kendall, 1968.

[65] Hutchinson-style bottles from Laconia's Cilley Bottling Works are also known to collectors. H.D. Cilley, proprietor, started this business sometime around 1900.

[66] "Granite State Spring, The New England States, New Hampshire." *American Mineral Waters*. W.W. Skinner, 1911, p.49.

[67] *A History of the American Soft Drink Industry, 1807-1957*. John J. Riley, 1972.

[68] Riley, 1972.

[69] Information regarding the Derry origins of Lafayette Beverage was complied from a number of historical sources, including: "Frederick Shepard Had an Earlier Version of the Right Stuff" and "General's Visit to Derry Gave Rise to Spring Water Enterprise," both by Rick Holmes, *Derry News*, 2010 and 2014 respectively.

[70] Although a water analysis by the U.S. Bureau of Agriculture in 1907 would reveal that, like so many other natural springs in New England, the water of Crystal Spring was relatively pure and safe for consumption, but otherwise unremarkable in its mineral composition. Its flow was reported to be a modest 3 gallons per minute at that time.

[71] Abbott may have had an existing business relationship with the owners, as one report indicated he was a chemist by training and had developed some flavorings for the company's carbonated beverages.

[72] One of those location was at 10 West Broadway, now the site of the Abbott House, a residence for the elderly and disabled.

[73] Apparently at this time LeMay became a co-owner of the Green Mountain Ginger Ale Company. That bottler operated at various locations in the city of Manchester until around 1950.

[74] In the early 1950s Moxie moved out of its Boston production facility to a compact operation in Needham Heights where it made concentrate and shifted to a dependency on contract bottlers like Lafayette Beverages.

[75] Marc Jolicoeur was interviewed by phone in February 2020 and followed up with extensive email exchanges. He provided company documents and a number of

original black & white photographs of the Lafayette operations, several of which appear in this chapter.

[76] Marc Jolicoeur relates one notable litigation in the 1970s when he had to defend his company against a product adulteration claim made by a painter of customized panel vans who called himself the "Mad Vanner." Suspiciously, the court suit alleged that turpentine (a common paint-thinner) was found in one of Lafayette's bottled products!

[77] "Worldwide Ingredients in Cott Beverages." *Nashua Telegraph*, March 25, 1948.

[78] *Manchester, the Queen City*, Manchester Chamber of Commerce, 1955.

[79] Cott Beverages were quite popular in the New Hampshire Lakes Region, especially in the Weirs Beach area. In the 1950s two giant rooftop Cott signs could be seen from the famous boardwalk – one on the Half-Moon Restaurant across the street and the other on The Superette convenient store just up the street.

[80] Accessed sources include: cullinarylore.com/drinks:what-was-the-first-diet-soda/, americanheritage.com/sweet-nothing-triump-diet-soda-0#1, foodtimeline.org/foodbeverages.

[81] Evangelos "Van" Demetriades shared his reflections and remembrances of working at Cott Beverages primarily via email correspondence in December 2019 and early 2020.

[82] Information related to Eugene Emerson was compiled from several historical sources including: "Milton Mills Druggist Eugene W. Emerson (1856-1927)" by Muriel Bristol. *Milton Observer*, December 19, 2021.

[83] "Bottling Firm Sends Tonic to Soldiers." *Portsmouth Herald*, October 17, 1942.

[84] Patricia LeFrancois related her childhood memories of collecting soda bottles to turn in for spending money via email correspondence on November 30, 2019.

[85] "Lucky Strike Ginger Ale Co." *Nashua Telegraph*, August 24, 1950. "Lucky Strike Beverages For That Real Fruit Tang." *Nashua Telegraph*, 1951.

[86] "Soft-drink Firm Owner: We Use Real Returnable Bottles." *Nashua Telegraph*, September 19, 1985.

[87] Polar Beverages trace their history back to a spring water company founded in 1882. Purchased by Dennis Crowley, it has remained a family business to this day, building on heritage recipes such as Polar Orange Dry and Birch Beer. Flavored

seltzers started in the 1970s, and Polar now regularly offers at least eighteen flavors plus seasonal specialties.

[88] "Bubble, Toil and Trouble: Do You Know the Full 115-Year History of SodaStream?" Abram Brown, forbes.com/, August 20, 2018; "SodaStream," *Wikipedia*, wikipedia.org/wiki/SodaStream, accessed February 17, 2023.

[89] "How Bottled Water Became America's Most Popular Beverage." *Robert Moss*, seriouseasts.com, First published July 2017 and updated March 7, 2023.

[90] Moss, 2023.

[91] "Birth of the Bottled Water Industry." Natraj Pandal, blog.bccresearch.com, August 10, 2018.

[92] Municipal tap waters are almost universally chlorinated for bacterial control at the treatment plants and transported throughout the delivery system before reaching the consumer's tap. This treatment for sanitary purposes can impart a taste and odor than many find unpleasant or even unpalatable. Since warm temperatures influence bacterial growth, water systems located in warmer climate zones can be affected year around whereas those in more temperate regions may just experience taste or odor issues during the summer months.

[93] I admit to certain personal preferences when it comes to bottled waters and have a difficult time paying for those that are simply filtered/purified tap waters–just on principle. I also don't care much for the highly mineralized/hard waters from high pH limestone aquifers, as many consumers certainly do. I am fond of soft, low TSD, granite-derived spring water (without actually naming brands!).

[94] Monadnockspring.com. Accessed November 10, 2022 and March 28, 2023.

[95] Crystalgeyserplease.com. Accessed August 2, 2022 and March 28, 2023.

[96] *Spy Capitalism – ITEK and the CIA* by Jonathan E. Lewis chronicles the full story.

[97] The majority of information for the company's profile came from in-person interviews with former Twin Mountain employees, Jeff Tamplin and Dave Wilson. The interviews took place in January and February 2020 and follow up with email correspondence in February 2022.

[98] Not to be confused with Glacier Mist, a current Wisconsin-based product or Glacier Clear, a current Minneapolis-based product, neither affiliated with The Coca-Cola Company or its bottlers.

[99] "Guzzlers Bring New Gear to Twin Mountain." Pat Reynolds, *Packaging World*, October 31, 1999.

[100] I am employed part-time by Worthen Industries in their quality and sustainability group and work there with two former Twin Mountain employees from their maintenance staff.

[101] "2021 State of the Beverage Industry: CSD's benefit from familiarity, flavor choices." Barbara Harfmann, bevindustry.com, July 1, 2021.

[102] Much of the history of Coca-Cola operations in New Hampshire was compiled from numerous published sources including the company's current website (cokenortheast.com) and its previous website (ccnne,com) prior to 2018.

[103] Correspondence with Dan Hovey of the Pease Greeter group, February 8, 2023.

[104] Additional information and fact-checking was obtained in email correspondence with Coca-Cola Beverages Northeast's Senior Director of Public Affairs, Susannah Smith in March 2022.

[105] "Moxie, 'An Acquired Taste,' Acquired by Coca-Cola." ABC Staff, American Botanical Council, Issue 120, Fall 2018. Accessed March 5, 2022.

[106] Most of the history of Private Label Specialties was compiled from published sources including the company's website (plspecialties.com) and from an extensive phone interview with owner Ray Duhaime on March 11, 2022 and associated follow-on email correspondence.

[107] Information for the Conner Bottling Works history was compiled from numerous published sources including: "An Old-time Treat: Squamscot Soda Enjoying Resurgence." Jesse Scardina, *Foster Daily Democrat*, September 20, 1915; "Squamscot Soda: Helping You Wash It All Down Since 1863." Todd Bookman, *New Hampshire Public Radio*, November 23, 2016; and *The History of Squamscot Soda*. Exeter Historical Society program video, accessed March 17, 2022. Information was also obtained from the company website (nhsoda.com) and from personal interviews conducted at the Newfields bottling site on March 4, 2022 and April 14, 2022.

SELECT BIBLIOGRAPHY

Allen, Frederick. Secret Formula, How Brilliant Marketing and Relentless Salesmanship Made Coca-Cola the Best-Known Brand in the World. Harper Business, 1994.

Anonymous. The American Bottler. New York, NY. The American Bottlers Publishing Co., Vol. XXXII, No. 1, January 15, 1912.

___. "Moxie Co. v. Daoust, No. 1,006". St. Paul, MN. The Federal Reporter, Vol. 206, Circuit Courts of Appeals, District Courts, and Commerce Courts of the United States. West Publishing Co., September-October 1913.

Back, William, Edward R. Landa, and Lisa Meeks. "Bottled Waters, Spas, and Early Years of Water Chemistry." Ground Water, Vol. 33, No.4, July-August 1995.

Blum, Deborah. The Poison Squad. Penguin Press, 2018.

Bowers, David Q. The Moxie Encyclopedia, Volume 1, The History. Vestal, NY. The Vestal Press, Ltd., 1985.

Brouder, Edward W. Jr., and Maurice B. Quirin. Manchester's Airport: Flying Through Time. Amherst, NH, United Business Technologies Press, 2006.

Brown, O. Phelps (Dr.). The Complete Herbalist, or the People Their Own Physicians by the Use of Nature's Remedies. Jersey City, NJ, Published by the author, 1866.

Brown, Walter A. Lithium: A Doctor, A Drug, and a Breakthrough. Liveright Publishing Co., 2019.

Chapelle, Frank. Wellsprings: A Natural History of Bottled Spring Waters. Rutgers University Press, 2005.

Chester, Thomas. Carbonated Beverages: The Art of Making, Dispensing, & Bottling Soda-Water, Mineral Waters, Ginger-Ale & Sparkling-Liquors. New York. P.H. Reilly, 1882.

Cramp, Arthur J. Nostrums and Quackery. American Medical Association, 1921.

Crook, James K. The Mineral Waters of the United States and their Therapeutic Uses. New York and Philadelphia. Lea Brothers & Co., 1899.

DeCorse, Christopher R. "Elixirs, Nerve Tonics and Panaceas: The Medicine Trade in Nineteenth-century New Hampshire." Historical New Hampshire. New Hampshire Historical Society, Vol. 39, Nos. 1-2, 1984.

Dietz, Lawrence. Soda Pop: The History, Advertising, Art and Memorabilia of Soft Drinks in America. Simon and Schuster, 1973.

Donovan, Tristan. Fizz: How Soda Shook Up the World. Chicago Review Press, Inc., 2014.

Duncan, Charles. Twenty-sixth Report of the State Board of Health of the State of New Hampshire for the Fiscal Period Ending August 31, 1920. Concord, NH, Rumford Printing Company, 1920.

Ebert, Albert E. and A. Emil Hiss. The Standard Formulary. Chicago, G.P. Engelhard & Company, 1899.

Emmis, Colin. Soft Drinks: Their Origin and History. Haverfordwest, Dyfed, Great Britain. Shire Publications Ltd., 1991.

Erlbach, Arlene. Soda Pop: How It's Made. Lerner Publications Company, 1994.

Estes, J. Worth. "The Shakers and Their Proprietary Medicines." Bulletin of the History of Medicine, V.65, No. 2 (Summer 1991). Johns Hopkins University Press,1991, pp. 162-184.

Farrow, Peter. The Yankee Trivia Book. Augusta, ME, Lance Tapley Publisher, 1985.

Ferraro, Pat & Bob Ferraro. The Past in Glass. Sparks, NV, Western Printing & Publishing Co., 1964.

Fewless, Dennis G. and Christopher A. Weide. Soft Drink Bottlers of the United States, Volume 1, Vermont & New Hampshire. Charleston, South Carolina, Platform 3 Research, Inc., Second Edition, 2014.

Freeman, Dr. Larry. Grand Old American Bottles. Watkins Glen, NY, Century House, 1964.

Gifford, George E. "Botanic Remedies in Colonial Massachusetts, 1620-1820." Medicines in Colonial Massachusetts, 1620-1820. Vol. 57, The Colonial Society of Massachusetts. University Press of Virginia,1980.

Hall, Elizabeth B. Canterbury Shaker Village: Medicines As Seen Through Archeological Artifacts. 2007. Plymouth State University, Master of Heritage Studies dissertation.

Hiss, A. Emil. The Standard Manual of Soda and Other Beverages. Chicago, G.P. Engelhard & Company, 1897.

Holbrook, Stewart H. The Golden Age of Quackery. The Macmillian Company, 1959.

Holmes, Richard D. "Frederick Shepard Had an Earlier Version of the Right Stuff." The Derry News, September 22, 2010.

___. "General's Visit to Derry Gave Rise to Spring Water Enterprise." The Derry News, July 31, 2014.

Huling, Charles C. (aka "Perfecto"). Notes on American Confectionery. Philadelphia, Self-published, 1891.

Jacobs, Morris B. Manufacturer and Analysis of Carbonated Beverages. New York, Chemical Publishing Co., Inc., 1959.

Katz, Josh. Speaking American – A Visual Guide. Boston & New York, Mariner Books, 2020.

Kendall, A. Harold. "Business & Industry." Upper Ashuelot, A History of Keene, New Hampshire. Keene History Commission, 1968. Accessed through the Keene Public Library digital files at keenenh.gove/keene-publiclibrary/.

Levin, Judith. Soda and Fizzy Drinks: A Global History. India, Replika Press Pvt. Ltd., 2021.

Lewis, Jonathan E. Spy Capitalism – ITEK and the CIA. New Haven and London, Yale University Press, 2002.

Lofland, Cheryl Harris. The National Soft Drink Association: A Tradition of Service. Washington, D.C., National Soft Drink Association, 1986.

Manchester Chamber of Commerce. Manchester the Queen City. Manchester, NH, 1955.

Mason, Walter. "Strongest Glass in the Country." Yankee Magazine, Vol. 33, May 1969, pp. 142-147.

Medbery, Henry E. The Manufacture of Bottled Carbonated Beverages. American Bottlers of Carbonated Beverages, 1945.

Moore, Richard B. Quality of Water in the Fractured Bedrock Aquifer of New Hampshire. U.S. Geological Survey Scientific Investigations Report 2002-5093, 2004.

Morrissey, D.J., John M. Regan. New Hampshire Ground-Water Quality. U.S. Geological Survey Open-File Report 87-0739, 1987.

Moss, Robert. "How the South Cornered the Soda Market." Seriouseats.com, updated August 10, 2018.

Munsey, Cecil. The Illustrated Guide to Collecting Bottles. Hawthorne Books, 1970.

Nickell, Joe. "Pop Culture: Patent Medicines Become Soda Drinks." Skeptical Inquirer, Vol. 35, No. 1, 2011. Accessed at: https://skepticalinquirer.org/2011/01/pop_culture_patent_med icines_become_soda_drinks/

Oppenheim, Janet. "Nerve Tonics and Treatments." Shattered Nerves: Doctors, Patients, and Depression in Victorian England. Chapter 4, Oxford University Press. 1991.

Pendergrast, Mark. For God, Country & Coca Cola. Basic Books, 2013.

Proper, David R. "The Lyndeborough Glass Company 1866 – 1886." Yankee Glass: A History of Glassmaking in New Hampshire 1790 – 1886, edited by John F. Bemis, The Yankee Bottle Club, Keene, New Hampshire, 1990, pp. 49-55.

Richards, David L. Poland Spring – A Tale of the Gilded Age, 1860-1900. Lebanon, NH, University of New Hampshire Press, 2005.

Riley, John J. Organization in the Soft Drink Industry: A History of the American Bottlers of Carbonated Beverages. American Bottlers of Carbonated Beverages, 1946.

___. A History of the American Soft Drink Industry, Bottled Carbonated Beverages 1807 – 1957. American Bottlers of Carbonated Beverages, 1958. Arno Press, 1972.

Robertson, Patricia. Robertson's Books of Firsts: Who Did What for the First Time. Bloomsbury USA, 2011.

Sasseville, Dennis and Merrill Lewis. Moxie. Images of America series, Arcadia Publishing, 2019.

Scribner, Vaughn. "'The Happy Effects of These Waters': Colonial American Mineral Spas and the British Civilizing Mission." Early American Studies: An Interdisciplinary Journal, Vol. 14, No. 3, Summer 2016, pp.409-449.

___. "Drowning in Health: Murky Perceptions of Mineral Water and Alcohol in Eighteenth-Century Medical Literature and Social Mores." Spa Culture and Literature in England, 1500-1800, edited by S. Chiari and S. Cuisinier-Delorme, Cham, Switzerland, Palgrave Macmillian, 2021.

Seagrave, Kerry. Vending Machines: An American Social History. Jefferson, NC and London, McFarland & Company, Inc., 2002.

Skinner, W.W. American Mineral Waters: The New England States. U.S. Department of Agriculture, Bureau of Chemistry, 1911.

Starbuck, David R. (Ed). Canterbury Shaker Village. New Hampshire Historical Society, Historical New Hampshire Special Issue, Vol. 48 Nos. 2 & 3, Summer/Fall 1993.

Stoddard, S.R. Saratoga Springs, Its Mineral Waters. Glen Falls, NY, Self-published, 1806, (reprinted 1897).

Sulz, Charles H. A Treatise on Beverages or The Complete Practical Bottler. New York, Dich & Fitzgerald Publishers, 1888.

Select Bibliography

Tchudi, Stephen A. Soda Poppery: The History of Soft Drinks in America. Charles Scribner's Sons, 1986.

Thall, David. Thall's Home Remedies. Manchester, NH, 1936. Accessed in the Manchester Historic Association's research library August 11, 2021.

The Scientific American Cyclopedia Receipts, Notes and Queries. Hopkins, edited by A. Albert. New York, Munn & Co. Publishers, 1892.

Tollison, Robert D., David P. Kaplan, and Richard S. Higgins. Competition and Concentration: The Economics of the Carbonated Soft Drink Industry. Lexington Books, 1985.

Wade, Rufus R. Report of the Chief of Massachusetts District Police for the Year Ending December 31, 1894. Results of the Inspection of Factories and Public Buildings. Boston, Wright and Potter Printing Co., 1895.

Watson, Irving A. Twentieth Report of the State Board of Health of the State of New Hampshire for the Fiscal Period Ending August 31, 1908. Rumford Printing Company, 1908.

Whitcher, Mary. Mary Witcher's Shaker House-Keeping. Shaker Village, NH, March 1, 1882, 1st ed. Accessed on Wikicource.org, June 12, 2022.

Wiley, Harvey W. Beverages and Their Adulteration. P. Blakinton's Sons & Co., 1919.

Witzel, Michael Karl, and Gyvel Young-Witzel. Soda Pop! From Miracle Medicine to Pop Culture. Town Square Books, Voyager Press, Inc., 1998.

Wright, Karen. The Road to Dr Pepper, Texas – The Story of Dublin Dr Pepper. Abilene, TX, State House Press, 2006.

Yates, Donald. "Ginger Beer and Root Beer Heritage." Bottles and Extras, Federation of Historic Bottle Collectors, Spring 2003, pp. 14-17.

___. "The First American Soda Fountains." Bottles and Extras, Federation of Historic Bottle Collectors, Spring 2006, pp. 70-73.

___. "Charles E. Hires Company, 1870-Present, Philadelphia, Pennsylvania." Bottles and Extras, Federation of Historic Bottle Collectors, Summer 2006, pp. 50-57.

Resource Organizations

Beverage Marketing Corporation, beveragemarketing.com.

International Bottled Water Association (IBWA), bottledwater.org.

Matthew Museum of Maine Heritage – Moxie Wing. Union, Maine. George Gross, Curator, Matthewsmuseum.org # ACKNOWLEDGEMENTS

This book represents a three-plus year effort starting with basic research and data collection. Along the way numerous individuals provided critical input that helped to shape the extensive story of New Hampshire spring water and flavored tonics/sodas. Ed Brouder (communications consultant) shared his knowledge of Manchester's former Cohas Springs operations, and Steve Young of Imageability did the same for both Cohas Springs and Londonderry Lithia Spring. Marc Jolicoeur (former part owner and President of Lafayette Beverages) provided personalized company insights as well as vintage photographs. Merrill Lewis (of the New England Moxie Congress) helped with assuring the accuracy of the book's Moxie references. Evangelos Demetriades shared his detailed recollections as a worker in Manchester's Cott Bottling plant. Founder Ray Duhaime shared insights of his successful Goffstown-based Private Label Specialties. The always-friendly folks at the Conner Bottling Works in Newfields shared the history of their family-owned business and allowed me to visit on multiple occasions.

A special thanks goes out to fellow-employees Jeff Tamplin and Dave Wilson for sharing information on the inner workings of the former Twin Mountain Spring Water Company. Susannah Smith and others at Coca-Cola Beverages Northeast provided key details on their Londonderry, New Hampshire operations. Dan Peters, formerly of the Manchester Historic Association's research team, provided extensive support and access to research files. Friends Susan Byrd and Patricia LeFrancois generously shared soda-related stories from their youth to help complement the author's own remembrances of earlier times.

I also wanted to acknowledge the assistance I received in getting this book from page to production. Erin Palazzo, Milt Dentch and Kathryn Sasseville provided critical (but kind) editing of the text. Dennis Magee and Milt Dentch offered sage advice on the self-publishing process, and Nadene Seiters of Self-Publishing Genie did masterful work in formatting and indexing my manuscript for final publication.

Most of all I want to acknowledge the unending support of my wife, Kathy, for her patience and love as I worked through this writing project.

Dennis Sasseville

July 2023

INDEX